"This series is a tremendous resource for those understanding of how the gospel is woven th. pastors and scholars doing gospel business from all the Scriptures. This is a biblical and theological feast preparing God's people to apply the entire Bible to all of life with heart and mind wholly committed to Christ's priorities."

BRYAN CHAPELL, President Emeritus, Covenant Theological Seminary; Senior Pastor, Grace Presbyterian Church, Peoria, Illinois

"Mark Twain may have smiled when he wrote to a friend, 'I didn't have time to write you a short letter, so I wrote you a long letter.' But the truth of Twain's remark remains serious and universal, because well-reasoned, compact writing requires extra time and extra hard work. And this is what we have in the Crossway Bible study series *Knowing the Bible*. The skilled authors and notable editors provide the contours of each book of the Bible as well as the grand theological themes that bind them together as one Book. Here, in a 12-week format, are carefully wrought studies that will ignite the mind and the heart."

R. KENT HUGHES, Visiting Professor of Practical Theology, Westminster Theological Seminary

"*Knowing the Bible* brings together a gifted team of Bible teachers to produce a high-quality series of study guides. The coordinated focus of these materials is unique: biblical content, provocative questions, systematic theology, practical application, and the gospel story of God's grace presented all the way through Scripture."

PHILIP G. RYKEN, President, Wheaton College

"These *Knowing the Bible* volumes provide a significant and very welcome variation on the general run of inductive Bible studies. This series provides substantial instruction, as well as teaching through the very questions that are asked. *Knowing the Bible* then goes even further by showing how any given text links with the gospel, the whole Bible, and the formation of theology. I heartily endorse this orientation of individual books to the whole Bible and the gospel, and I applaud the demonstration that sound theology was not something invented later by Christians, but is right there in the pages of Scripture."

GRAEME L. GOLDSWORTHY, former lecturer, Moore Theological College; author, *According to Plan, Gospel and Kingdom, The Gospel in Revelation*, and *Gospel and Wisdom*

"What a gift to earnest, Bible-loving, Bible-searching believers! The organization and structure of the Bible study format presented through the *Knowing the Bible* series is so well conceived. Students of the Word are led to understand the content of passages through perceptive, guided questions, and they are given rich insights and application all along the way in the brief but illuminating sections that conclude each study. What potential growth in depth and breadth of understanding these studies offer! One can only pray that vast numbers of believers will discover more of God and the beauty of his Word through these rich studies."

BRUCE A. WARE, Professor of Christian Theology, The Southern Baptist Theological Seminary

KNOWING THE BIBLE

J. I. Packer, Theological Editor
Dane C. Ortlund, Series Editor
Lane T. Dennis, Executive Editor

•   •   •   •   •   •

Genesis	Psalms	Jonah, Micah, and Nahum	Ephesians
Exodus	Proverbs		Philippians
Leviticus	Ecclesiastes	Haggai, Zechariah, and Malachi	Colossians and Philemon
Numbers	Song of Solomon		
Deuteronomy	Isaiah	Matthew	1–2 Thessalonians
Joshua	Jeremiah	Mark	1–2 Timothy and Titus
Judges	Lamentations, Habakkuk, and Zephaniah	Luke	
Ruth and Esther		John	Hebrews
1–2 Samuel		Acts	James
1–2 Kings	Ezekiel	Romans	1–2 Peter and Jude
1–2 Chronicles	Daniel	1 Corinthians	1–3 John
Ezra and Nehemiah	Hosea	2 Corinthians	Revelation
Job	Joel, Amos, and Obadiah	Galatians	

•   •   •   •   •   •

J. I. PACKER is Board of Governors' Professor of Theology at Regent College (Vancouver, BC). Dr. Packer earned his DPhil at the University of Oxford. He is known and loved worldwide as the author of the best-selling book *Knowing God*, as well as many other titles on theology and the Christian life. He serves as the General Editor of the ESV Bible and as the Theological Editor for the *ESV Study Bible*.

LANE T. DENNIS is President of Crossway, a not-for-profit publishing ministry. Dr. Dennis earned his PhD from Northwestern University. He is Chair of the ESV Bible Translation Oversight Committee and Executive Editor of the *ESV Study Bible*.

DANE C. ORTLUND is Executive Vice President of Bible Publishing and Bible Publisher at Crossway. He is a graduate of Covenant Theological Seminary (MDiv, ThM) and Wheaton College (BA, PhD). Dr. Ortlund has authored several books and scholarly articles in the areas of Bible, theology, and Christian living.

JUDGES

A 12-WEEK STUDY

Miles V. Van Pelt

:: CROSSWAY®

WHEATON, ILLINOIS

Knowing the Bible: Judges, A 12-Week Study

Copyright © 2018 by Crossway

Published by Crossway
    1300 Crescent Street
    Wheaton, Illinois 60187

All rights reserved. No part of this publication may be reproduced, stored in a retrieval system, or transmitted in any form by any means, electronic, mechanical, photocopy, recording, or otherwise, without the prior permission of the publisher, except as provided for by USA copyright law. Crossway® is a registered trademark in the United States of America.

Some content used in this study guide has been adapted from the *ESV Study Bible*, copyright © 2008 by Crossway, pages 433–474. Used by permission. All rights reserved.

Cover design: Simplicated Studio

First printing 2018

Printed in the United States of America

Scripture quotations are from the ESV® Bible (The Holy Bible, English Standard Version®), copyright © 2001 by Crossway, a publishing ministry of Good News Publishers. Used by permission. All rights reserved.

All emphases in Scripture quotations have been added by the author.

Trade paperback ISBN: 978-1-4335-5729-3
EPub ISBN: 978-1-4335-5732-3
PDF ISBN: 978-1-4335-5730-9
Mobipocket ISBN: 978-1-4335-5731-6

Crossway is a publishing ministry of Good News Publishers.

VP		28	27	26	25	24	23	22	21	20	19	18
15	14	13	12	11	10	9	8	7	6	5	4	3	2	1

TABLE OF CONTENTS

SERIES PREFACE

KNOWING THE BIBLE, as the series title indicates, was created to help readers know and understand the meaning, the message, and the God of the Bible. Each volume in the series consists of 12 units that progressively take the reader through a clear, concise study of one or more books of the Bible. In this way, any given volume can fruitfully be used in a 12-week format either in group study, such as in a church-based context, or in individual study. Of course, these 12 studies could be completed in fewer or more than 12 weeks, as convenient, depending on the context in which they are used.

Each study unit gives an overview of the text at hand before digging into it with a series of questions for reflection or discussion. The unit then concludes by highlighting the gospel of grace in each passage ("Gospel Glimpses"), identifying whole-Bible themes that occur in the passage ("Whole-Bible Connections"), and pinpointing Christian doctrines that are affirmed in the passage ("Theological Soundings").

The final component to each unit is a section for reflecting on personal and practical implications from the passage at hand. The layout provides space for recording responses to the questions proposed, and we think readers need to do this to get the full benefit of the exercise. The series also includes definitions of key words. These definitions are indicated by a note number in the text and are found at the end of each chapter.

Lastly, to help understand the Bible in this deeper way, we urge readers to use the ESV Bible and the *ESV Study Bible*, which are available in various print and digital formats, including online editions at esv.org. The *Knowing the Bible* series is also available online.

May the Lord greatly bless your study as you seek to know him through knowing his Word.

J. I. Packer
Lane T. Dennis

WEEK 1: OVERVIEW

▲

Why would Christians study a book like Judges, a book that would easily be rated R for its content if produced for the modern screen? Death and slaughter, human sacrifice and betrayal, illicit sex and scandal saturate the pages of this book. Ehud murders Eglon and leaves him to rot in his own fecal matter. Jephthah sacrifices his only daughter as a burnt offering because of a vow he has made to the Lord. Samson spends a night with a prostitute. A Levite cuts up his concubine, who has been brutally raped to death, and sends her dismembered body throughout Israel in order to incite war. In the book of Judges, we observe clearly that life is messy and foul and complicated, and that it is the cycle of our own sin that creates these problems.

Because of the startling nature of these narratives, it might seem like the book of Judges lacks a content filter, but this is not true. In John 5:39, we are taught that Jesus is the filter through which we must read the book of Judges. Christ states, "You search the Scriptures because you think that in them you have eternal life; *and it is they [the Old Testament Scriptures] that bear witness about me.*" The narratives contained in the book of Judges were written to "bear witness" or "testify" to the person and work of Jesus and the great salvation he has achieved for his people.

The most shocking feature in the book of Judges, therefore, is not the horror of the people's sin depicted in these narratives but the glory of salvation from that sin, accomplished by the God of patience, mercy, compassion, steadfast love, and faithfulness (Ex. 34:6). The terror of sin is outshone only by the glory of God's salvation worked through these judges, who then point us to Jesus Christ. This is just how the book of Hebrews teaches us to read the book of Judges:

> And what more shall I say? For time would fail me to tell of *Gideon, Barak, Samson, Jephthah,* of David and Samuel and the prophets—who *through faith* conquered kingdoms, enforced justice, obtained promises, stopped the mouths of lions, quenched the power of fire, escaped the edge of the sword, were made strong out of weakness, became mighty in war, put foreign armies to flight. (Heb. 11:32–34)

These judges were "commended through their faith" (Heb. 11:39) and are now part of that "great . . . cloud of witnesses" that calls us to "[look] to Jesus, the founder and perfecter of our faith" (Heb. 12:1–2). And so, we are moved to study this often-neglected book of the Bible because it teaches us about God's great salvation in Christ for his people from our incessant inclination to forget him, his promises, and all of the good blessings encountered in covenant life.

▶ Placing Judges in the Larger Story

The book of Judges describes a period in the life of the nation of Israel between the prophetic leadership of Moses and Joshua and the establishment of the monarchy. The nature of this time period is described on four different occasions in the book: "In those days there was no king in Israel. Everyone did what was right in his own eyes" (Judg. 17:6; compare 18:1; 19:1; 21:25). This brief summary statement teaches us two important facts about the period of the judges in Israel: (1) there was a crisis of leadership; and (2) there was, consequently, a crisis in Israel's faithfulness to their covenant with the Lord.

The wilderness generation of Moses and the generation of conquest under Joshua had been eyewitnesses of God's great signs and wonders to save and deliver. But then "there arose another generation after them who did not know the LORD or the work that he had done for Israel" (Judg. 2:10). In the generations between Joshua and the kings, Israel did "what was evil in the sight of the LORD" (v. 11). The evil described in the book of Judges should be understood as Israel's progressive decline into idolatry. The nation of Israel was originally called by God to be a "kingdom of priests and a holy nation" (Ex. 19:6), but by the end of the book of Judges, Israel has become like all the other nations around them and, even worse, like Sodom and Gomorrah (see Judges 19; compare Genesis 19).

By the end of the book, like the author himself we find ourselves looking for the king who will be able finally to deliver God's people from sin and corruption, who will give rest to God's people, and who will establish their inheritance in the land forever. The judges in the book of Judges, like the kings after them, cause us to look forward to the coming of the King of kings. Together, we look for that king who does not do what is "right in his own eyes" but who delights to do the will of his Father in heaven (John 6:38–40).

Major themes we will encounter in the book of Judges include:

- The important connection between Israel's obedience to the covenant and her possession (or forfeiture) of the land of inheritance.
- The importance of biblical leadership to promote faithfulness to God's law and to establish the land's rest from foreign oppression.
- The unending grace and mercy of God, demonstrated by the raising up of faithful judges through whom he rescues and saves his people.
- The trap of idolatry that promises freedom but results in oppression and subjugation.
- The corruption of idolatry that twists us into what we falsely worship.
- The power of God to rescue his people from the worst types of sin, idolatry, and oppression.

Key Verses

"In those days there was no king in Israel. Everyone did what was right in his own eyes." (Judg. 17:6; compare 18:1; 19:1; 21:25)

Date and Historical Background

The book of Judges occupies the time between the death of Joshua (Judg. 1:1; 2:8) and Samuel's ministry of establishing the monarchy in Israel (1 Samuel 8)—approximately 1360 to 1084 BC. These are dark days in the life of Israel, characterized by sin, idolatry, foreign oppression, and national corruption. But it is against this dark backdrop that the glory of God's faithfulness shines as he continues to save and deliver his people from their sin.

In this book we encounter a host of nations that surround and subsequently oppress Israel: the Philistines, Midianites, Moabites, Ammonites, Amorites, Canaanites, Hittites, Jebusites, and others. Some of these nations are even related to Israel through Abraham (e.g., the Moabites), adding insult to injury.

For most of the judges, the duration of their service and the tribe in Israel from which they originate is described in the text. However, the accounts of the judges likely do not appear in chronological order, nor are they necessarily arranged geographically. It seems, rather, that the accounts are arranged to portray Israel's progressive spiral downward into idolatry as they increasingly become like the Canaanites they had been called to exterminate from the land.

Outline

The book of Judges includes two introductions, two conclusions, 12 judges (six major judges and six minor judges), and one anti-judge, Abimelech. The judges are presented in two parts, according to the six major judges. The first of the major judges are Othniel, Ehud, and Deborah/Barak, and then Gideon, Jephthah, and Samson. In general, the accounts of the judges become progressively longer as the sin of Israel becomes progressively worse. As we traverse the accounts, we will also observe how the cost of deliverance for the judge increases as Israel's sin worsens.

I. Introduction to the Judges (1:1–3:6)

    A. The Crisis of Israel's Inheritance (*Land*) (1:1–36)

    B. The Crisis of Israel's Faith (*Idolatry*) (2:1–3:6)

II. The Judges (3:7–16:31)

    A. The First Three Major Judges (3:7–5:31)

        1. Othniel (*Major*) (3:7–11)
        2. Ehud (*Major*) (3:12–30)
        3. Shamgar (*Minor*) (3:31)
        4. Deborah/Barak (*Major*) (4:1–5:31)

    B. The Second Three Major Judges (6:1–16:31)

        1. Gideon (*Major*) (6:1–8:35)
        2. Abimelech (*Anti-Judge*) (9:1–57)
        3. Tola (*Minor*) (10:1–2)
        4. Jair (*Minor*) (10:3–5)
        5. Jephthah (*Major*) (10:6–12:7)
        6. Ibzan (*Minor*) (12:8–10)
        7. Elon (*Minor*) (12:11–12)
        8. Abdon (*Minor*) (12:13–15)
        9. Samson (*Major*) (13:1–16:31)

III. Conclusion to the Judges (17:1–21:25)

    A. The Crisis of Israel's Faith (*Idolatry*) (17:1–19:30)

    B. The Crisis of Israel's Inheritance (*Tribe*) (20:1–21:25)

As You Get Started

According to the book of Hebrews (Heb. 11:32–12:3), the book of Judges is not merely a morality play about good and bad decision making in life and what we can learn from the judges' deeds. It is an account of God's faithfulness to his people in spite of their constant faithlessness, as he sends deliverers, one after the other, to rescue his people from the calamities of their sin. How have you thought about these judges and the book of Judges in the past?

What are some of the major obstacles in your own thinking that keep you from understanding the judges as types (examples) of Christ and his saving work, over against thinking of them only as types (examples) of us as sinners in need of grace?

What do you hope to discover or learn as you study the book of Judges over the course of the next 12 weeks?

As You Finish This Unit . . .

Take a few minutes to ask for God's help to grasp the historical account and the significance of the book of Judges for the Christian life. Ask that you might understand how these narratives "bear witness" or "testify" to the person and work of Jesus Christ (John 5:39; Luke 24:27, 44). Prepare to encounter a God who is fierce to save his people from their sins as we consider the gospel "promised beforehand" (Rom. 1:2) in the book of Judges.

WEEK 2: INTRODUCING THE JUDGES, TWICE!

Judges 1:1–3:6

▲

The Place of the Passage

These opening chapters of Judges describe the national and theological condition of Israel following the death of Joshua. They set the scene for the coming of the judges in 3:7–16:31. In chapter 1, we read of Israel's relative failure to expel the inhabitants of the Promised Land. Then, in 2:1–3:6, we encounter the reasons for and consequences of that failure.

The Big Picture

With Moses and Joshua dead, the Lord raises up judges to deliver his people from foreign oppression caused by their own sin and idolatry. These judges lead Israel, promote covenantal obedience, and secure the land's rest from subjugation.

> **Reflection and Discussion**

Read through Judges 1:1–3:6, then engage this section of Scripture with the questions below. (For further background, see the *ESV Study Bible*, pages 439–443; available online at www.esv.org.)

1. The Account of Israel's Failure to Possess the Land Fully (1:1–36)

These opening verses describe the relative success and/or failure of the tribes of Israel to possess the land according to the command of the Lord (Deut. 7:1–5). It is important to observe that not all of the tribes of Israel are mentioned in this chapter, nor is each tribe described with the same level of detail. Using Exodus 1:1–5, write down the names of the 12 tribes of Israel and identify which tribes are missing from Judges 1:1–36. For the relationship between Joseph, Ephraim, and Manasseh, see Genesis 48:1–20.

Which of the tribes in Judges 1 is highlighted by the length of its account (vv. 2–20)? Why would the emphasis on this tribe be important, given the prominent theme of kingship at the end of the book (17:6; 18:1; 19:1; 21:25)?

In addition to the tribes of Israel (e.g., Judah, Simeon) and the people groups in the land (e.g., Canaanites, Jebusites), what individuals are mentioned by name in this chapter?

In 1:21, the relative success of Judah is contrasted with the failure of Benjamin to drive out the inhabitants of Jerusalem. How is the tribe of Benjamin further depicted in Judges 19, and how, once again, does this negative characterization relate to the important theme of kingship in the book of Judges? See 1 Samuel 9:1–2.

As we read chapter 1 of Judges, we will encounter a statement repeated several times, along the lines of, "So the Canaanites lived among them" (see vv. 21 ["Jebusites"], 29, 30, 32, and 33). Given what we already know about the book of Judges and the instruction from Deuteronomy 7:1–4, what is the danger in Israel's allowing these people to remain in the land?

2. The Reason Israel Failed to Fully Possess the Land (2:1–3:6)

In 2:1–5, the angel of the Lord indicts Israel for unfaithfulness to the Sinai (Mosaic) covenant. What has Israel done to break the covenant, and what is the punishment for their disobedience?

The death of Joshua is recorded twice in the book of Judges (1:1; 2:6–10). What is the significance of his death, and the death of that whole generation, for understanding the book of Judges?

Most of the judge narratives begin with a statement such as, "And the people of Israel did what was evil in the sight of the LORD" (2:11; compare 3:7, 12). What is this "evil," according to 2:11–13, and how does the Lord respond to these evil deeds?

In 2:16–23, the text explains why the Lord raises up the judges and what they do for Israel. What does the text say about these judges? Why does the Lord raise them up? What do they do for Israel?

When a judge dies, how does Israel respond? What do they do (2:19)?

According to 3:1–6, why does the Lord allow foreign nations to remain in the land of Israel? What is the result of Israel's living among those nations?

....

....

....

....

....

....

Read through the following three sections on *Gospel Glimpses, Whole-Bible Connections*, and *Theological Soundings*. Then take time to consider the *Personal Implications* these sections may have for you.

▶ Gospel Glimpses

WHY ADONAI-BEZEK? Sometimes it can be difficult to understand why certain events are recorded in Scripture. For example, why does the book of Judges open with the account of Adonai-bezek? Here, we encounter a self-styled "king of the world" (because he had conquered 70 kings) who is subjugated by Judah and then dies in Jerusalem. Adonai-bezek has something to teach us about his situation: "As I have done, so God has repaid me" (1:7). In order for God's people to possess their inheritance, a great king must die in Jerusalem. The inheritance of ethnic Israel was the land of Canaan, but the ultimate inheritance for the people of God is the land of the new heavens and the new earth. In order for us to possess this inheritance, we must be united by faith to the true King of the world, who was put to death in Jerusalem—but not for his own sins. As we have done (in *our* sin), so God has repaid *him*. "Therefore [Jesus] is the mediator of a new covenant, so that those who are called may receive the promised eternal inheritance, since a death has occurred that redeems them from the transgressions committed under the first covenant" (Heb. 9:15).

THE GOSPEL OF THE KENITES. The mention of the Kenites in Judges 1:16 reminds us that the promises God made to Abraham are still at work, even in the dark and difficult days of the judges. Yes, the nation of Israel was commissioned by God to exterminate the Canaanites because of their sin, and, as a kingdom of priests (Ex. 19:6), Israel was to purify the realm in which God would cause his name to dwell. But we are reminded by the Kenites that God's ultimate plan through Abraham's offspring is still operative, that "in [Abraham] all of the families of the earth shall be blessed" (Gen. 12:3). The inclusion of the Kenites in Judah is a picture of this gospel reality, just as the apostle Paul expresses in

Galatians 3:8: "The Scripture, foreseeing that God would justify the Gentiles by faith, preached the gospel beforehand to Abraham, saying, 'In you shall all the nations be blessed.'"

MOVED TO PITY. The author of Judges makes it clear that Israel's suffering and subjugation is the direct result of their own sin and idolatry (2:11–15). It is also clear that the Lord gives his people over to such suffering because of their sin (2:14). Thus we should be struck by the statement that "the LORD was moved to pity by their groaning because of those who afflicted and oppressed them" (2:18). The Lord does not abandon his people to sin. Rather, it is he who delivers us *from* our sin. We do not clean up our lives in order to become favored by God. It is just the opposite. Because God has favored us in Christ, we are empowered unto holy living as we worship the God of our salvation.

Whole-Bible Connections

AFTER THE DEATH OF JOSHUA. The opening line in the book of Judges is nearly identical to the opening line of the book of Joshua, which begins, "After the death of Moses." By beginning in this way, we come to understand that the book of Judges continues the narrative of Joshua, which is itself a continuation of the narrative of Deuteronomy. As such, we encounter the unity of the plan of God in the outworking of history across the ages. This is especially important for understanding the book of Judges, where it appears that God's plan and God's people are simply falling apart. But the Lord knows what he is doing. He has "[declared] the end from the beginning" (Isa. 46:10), and nothing catches him by surprise. Even Israel's fall into sin, idolatry, and subsequent exile is part of God's plan for redemption (see Deuteronomy 31).

PROBLEMATIC MARRIAGES. The second introduction to the book of Judges (2:1–3:6) concludes with a statement addressing Israel's proclivity to marry people from the nations around them: "Their daughters they took to themselves for wives, and their own daughters they gave to their sons, and they served their gods" (3:6). It is important to note the connection between intermarriage and idolatry in this concluding statement. A similar connection is found in Genesis 6, where intermarriage (vv. 1–2) and increasing wickedness (v. 5) serve as the prelude to God's judgment of the world in the flood. The same reality turns Solomon's heart away from God and results in the tearing apart of Israel into two nations (1 Kings 11:8–11; compare Deut. 7:1–6). We can understand, then, why Paul is so insistent that Christians must "not be unequally yoked with unbelievers. For what partnership has righteousness with lawlessness? Or what fellowship has light with darkness?" (2 Cor. 6:14). Marriage is a powerful, transforming, life-changing union. Praise God, then, for our everlasting union with Christ, our covenantal husband, and the transforming power of his holiness in us (Rev. 19:7; 21:2, 9; 22:17).

▶ Theological Soundings

ISRAEL, THE LAND, AND OBEDIENCE. Israel's occupation of the land is dependent upon their obedience to the Sinai (Mosaic) covenant (Deut. 30:15–18). The book of Judges teaches us that Israel is not obedient to that covenant (Judg. 2:2), and so their eventual expulsion from the land (loss of inheritance) is an act of the Lord's faithfulness to the Mosaic covenant, just as Adam was expelled from the garden of Eden for his disobedience to the covenant of works. But Adam's and Israel's disobedience is trumped by the obedience of Christ, which is for the benefit of all those who are united to him by faith (Rom. 4:13; James 2:5). As such, Christians are heirs to "an inheritance that is imperishable, undefiled, and unfading, kept in heaven for you" (1 Pet. 1:4).

INSTRUMENTS AND AGENT. Who saves whom? In our study of the book of Judges—or any part of the Bible, for that matter—it is always important to distinguish between the instruments and the agent of our salvation. This principle is well illustrated in the book of Judges. The Bible can speak of human saviors who deliver God's people, as in Judges 2:16: "Then the LORD raised up judges, who saved them out of the hand of those who plundered them." But a mere two verses later, the same verb is employed in relation to the Lord: "Whenever the LORD raised up judges for them, the LORD was with the judge, and he saved them from the hand of their enemies all the days of the judge" (2:18). It is the Lord who raises up these judges, and it is the Lord who empowers them by his Spirit. The Lord is the agent, the power, the will, and the force to save. The judge is simply a tool in the hand of the Lord, the true and better Judge (see 11:27).

▶ Personal Implications

Take time to reflect on the implications of Judges 1:1–3:6 for your life. How does this passage lead you to praise God, repent of sin, and trust more deeply in his gracious promises? Write down your reflections under the three headings we have considered and on the passage as a whole.

1. Gospel Glimpses

----

2. Whole-Bible Connections

3. Theological Soundings

4. Judges 1:1–3:6

As You Finish This Unit . . .

Take a few minutes to ask for God's help to grasp the significance of Judges 1:1–3:6 in terms of both God's work in history to accomplish such a great salvation and your own life as a part of that plan, as one who has been saved from the "plundering" (see 2:14) of the enemy.

Week 3: Othniel, Ehud, and Shamgar

Judges 3:7–31

The Place of the Passage

The book of Judges contains two introductions, two conclusions, 12 judges (six major judges and six minor judges), and one anti-judge (Abimelech). In 3:7–31, we encounter in rapid succession the first two major judges, Othniel and Ehud, and then Shamgar, the first of the so-called minor judges. Although these initial judge narratives are relatively brief, especially when compared to the accounts of Gideon, Jephthah, and Samson, they set the standard and establish the pattern for each of the following judges. Othniel shows us what to expect, while Ehud illustrates those expectations. It is also helpful to understand that the designation "minor" judge relates to the relative brevity of each account, ranging between one and three verses. The inclusion of six minor judges gives us 12 total judges, perhaps representing the number of tribes in Israel. These minor judges also appear at strategic locations in the overall narrative of the judges, perhaps signaling the appearance of a climactic judge narrative. In this way, Shamgar identifies the Deborah and Barak account as the climax of the first three major judges; Tola and Jair appear together and identify the climactic role of the Jephthah account; and, finally, Ibzan, Elon, and Abdon together distinguish Samson as the final, climactic judge in the book of Judges.

> ## The Big Picture

The judges raised up by the Lord are Spirit-endowed saviors who deliver God's people from the oppression and subjugation caused by their sin.

> ## Reflection and Discussion

Read through Judges 3:7–31, then engage this section of Scripture with the questions below. (For further background, see the *ESV Study Bible*, pages 443–444; available online at www.esv.org.)

1. Othniel, the Paradigmatic Judge (3:7–11)

The account of Othniel is the shortest of the major judge narratives, stretching only five verses. However, the Othniel narrative sets the pattern for all the other major judge narratives. This pattern includes seven basic parts: (1) Israel does evil in the eyes of the Lord; (2) the Lord sells/gives Israel into the hands of their enemy; (3) Israel cries out to the Lord because of their oppression at the hands of the enemy; (4) the Lord raises up a judge as savior/deliverer; (5) the Lord gives the enemy into the hands of the judge; (6) the land experiences rest during the life of the judge; and (7) the judge dies. Can you identify/reword all seven parts of this recurring judge cycle in verses 7–11 of the Othniel account?

The Othniel account also identifies three basic characteristics of a judge. A judge is one who (1) "judges," (2) "saves" or "delivers," and (3) is empowered by the Spirit of God. Only Othniel and Samson (the first and the last judge) receive all three descriptors. Can you locate these three descriptors in the Othniel account?

In 3:7 we read, "Israel did what was evil in the sight of the LORD." This statement is followed by two descriptions of the evil committed. What was the twofold evil Israel committed, according to verse 7?

Read Deuteronomy 8:11–20 and summarize the danger of what it means to "forget" the Lord in the context of Israel's covenantal relationship with God. What should Israel remember?

Read 2 Peter 1:1–9. What are Christians in danger of forgetting, which may hinder one's growth in grace?

2. Ehud, the Left-Handed Savior (3:12–30)

The account of Ehud is the only other judge account to exhibit all seven elements of the judge cycle identified in the Othniel narrative. Can you identify/reword each of the seven parts in 3:12–30?

The account of Ehud and Eglon is filled with interesting detail and description. For example, each man is described with one particular physical trait that plays a major role in the narrative (vv. 15, 17). What physical trait is specified for each man? Why are these traits important to the narrative?

The account of the assassination of Eglon is filled with humorous satire and ridicule in order to criticize Israel's subjugation to such a people. Can you identify the satirical features in the narrative?

3. Shamgar, the Philistine Assassin (3:31)

In what way is the account of Shamgar different from the accounts of Othniel and Ehud? In what way are these accounts the same? What specific characteristic of a judge is applied to Shamgar?

Read through the following three sections on *Gospel Glimpses*, *Whole-Bible Connections*, and *Theological Soundings*. Then take time to consider the *Personal Implications* these sections may have for you.

Gospel Glimpses

GOSPEL AMNESIA. Israel failed to remember that God had saved them out of bondage and slavery and had given them an undeserved inheritance. This state of affairs resulted in their idolatry, or, better, "gospel amnesia"—the failure to live in light of God's salvation and grace. Given the tendencies of our own hearts, how can we protect ourselves from forgetting the grace of God (see Gal. 2:11–16; 2 Pet. 1:9)? We must come to the only one who truly knows the Father, to the one who never forgot. Jesus said of himself, "No one knows the Son except the Father, and no one knows the Father except the Son *and anyone to whom the Son chooses to reveal him*" (Matt. 11:27). From this vantage point, Jesus' words on the cross take on their full significance: "My God, my God, why have you forsaken me?" (Matt. 27:46). The cosmic curse of our gospel amnesia was poured out on the only one who truly knows God. The Father had to forsake or "forget" the only one who had ever truly known him, in order that we might also come to know him in all his fullness, for all eternity, and without the possibility of ever forgetting the God of our great salvation.

QUICK TO SAVE. When the Lord proclaimed his name to Moses on Mount Sinai, he revealed that he is "slow to anger" (Ex. 34:6), but this does not mean that the Lord allows sin to go unpunished. The Lord not only is slow to anger; he also "will by no means clear the guilty" (Ex. 34:7). The repeated sin of Israel in the book of Judges provokes the Lord's anger (see Judg. 3:7–8), and he punishes his people for their sin (3:12). But when the people cry out to the Lord, we read that he is quick to save (3:9, 15). The punishment of the Lord is a means of grace in the life of Israel because it causes their hearts to return to the Lord and to experience again his salvation. Because of the suffering of Jesus on the cross for our sins, Christians will never experience the final judgment of God against sin. However, we do experience his fatherly discipline, much like Israel did in the days of the judges, and this is good news! "It is for discipline [not judgment] that you have to endure. God is treating you as sons" (Heb. 12:7).

Whole-Bible Connections

THE LORD STRENGTHENED EGLON. Sometimes it is difficult to understand how God works "all things ... for good" (see Rom. 8:28), but the account of Ehud and Eglon can help us to grasp how this might work. The account of Israel's subjugation by Moab is an act of God, not some geopolitical happenstance. The Lord strengthens (or hardens) Eglon and Moab against Israel because of Israel's sin. You may also recall that the Lord worked in the same way with Pharaoh when he was oppressing Israel in Egypt. It is recorded repeatedly in the book of Exodus that the Lord "hardened" (or "strengthened," same verb) the heart of Pharaoh against Israel (Ex. 7:13, 22; 8:19; 9:7, 12, 35; 10:20, 27; 11:10). In the case of both Pharaoh and Eglon, however, the hardening of the king's heart and the oppression of God's people led to the defeat of the enemy and the salvation of God's people. Though it may not always be clear to us, especially in the context of suffering and hardship, the Lord is always working *all* things for the good of his people.

JUDGES DIE. A repeated feature in most of the judge narratives is the land's rest for a period of time after the deliverance by the judge before the judge eventually dies. In fact, the death of leadership in the days of the judges is a big problem for Israel. Twice it is recorded that Joshua dies, and so does Othniel, Ehud, Gideon, Jephthah, and finally Samson. Every time a judge dies, Israel sins all the more and falls deeper and deeper into corruption. Perhaps this is one reason why Israel desires a king. With kingship and dynastic succession, Israel could secure and "ensure" its tenure in the land with continuous, uninterrupted leadership. The problem with this plan, however, will be that most of Israel's kings will turn out to be corrupt and will do that which is evil in the sight of God, leading the nation into idolatry and eventual exile. What God's people truly need is an immortal Savior who can secure the obedience of his people forever. So then, to Jesus, "to the King of the ages, immortal, invisible, the only God, be honor and glory forever and ever. Amen" (1 Tim. 1:17).

Theological Soundings

THE MEANS OF GRACE, AND HELP TO REMEMBER. A major theme in the book of Judges is Israel's repeated turning away from the Lord into idolatry, that is, "doing what is evil in the sight of the LORD." In fact, this is the only element of the judge cycle that is repeated in all six major judge narratives. It is what provokes to anger the God who is "slow to anger" (Ex. 34:6). In Judges 3:7, Israel's idolatry is the result of "forgetting" the Lord (Deut. 8:11–20). Under the old covenant, the Lord gave his people the signs of circumcision and Sabbath, along with the annual feasts, so that they would remember their salvation and the covenant with their Savior. In the new covenant, our God has also given us baptism and the Lord's Supper (Communion) as reminders. We have the Scriptures that make known to us our sin, the tyranny of sin's oppression, and the great salvation accomplished for us by Jesus Christ. We experience these means of grace when we gather together as God's people on the Lord's Day for worship, to hear his Word read and preached, to remember the gospel in prayer and praise, and to see his grace set forth in the sacraments of baptism and Communion. Let us then *remember* his gracious command to us, "Do this in remembrance of me" (Luke 22:19; compare 1 Cor. 11:24–26).

Personal Implications

Take time to reflect on the implications of Judges 3:7–31 for your life. How does this passage lead you to praise God, repent of sin, and trust more deeply in his gracious promises? Write down your reflections under the three headings we have considered and on the passage as a whole.

1. Gospel Glimpses

2. Whole-Bible Connections

3. Theological Soundings

4. Judges 3:7–31

As You Finish This Unit . . .

Take a few minutes to ask for God's help to grasp the significance of Othniel, Ehud, and Shamgar as saviors of God's people and types of Jesus, our ultimate Savior. How are we like the people of Israel in the book of Judges, forgetting God's grace and pursuing cheap idols? What are the cycles of sin that we experience in our own lives, and how has God graciously rescued us from the oppression of sin's cancerous grip on our lives? Cry out to the Lord, for he is ready and quick to save.

Week 4: Deborah and Barak—Double Trouble

Judges 4:1–5:31

As mentioned previously, the book of Judges contains two introductions, two conclusions, 12 judges (six major judges and six minor judges), and one anti-judge (Abimelech). The account of Deborah and Barak brings our first set of three major judges (Othniel, Ehud, Deborah/Barak) to a climax. The climactic nature of this narrative is showcased in part by all of the "doubles" featured in this account. For example, there are two leaders (Deborah and Barak), two villains (Jabin and Sisera), two leading women (Deborah and Jael), and even two different accounts of deliverance: the first in narrative style (ch. 4) and the second in poetic song (ch. 5). The Samson narratives also exhibit this double structure (chs. 13–15 and then ch. 16), marking the third and sixth judge narratives as climactic accounts in the book of Judges. This same structure is reflected in Genesis 1 and the days of creation, as days 3 and 6 are double creation narratives.

There is, however, an important difference between the presentations in Genesis 1 and Judges. In Genesis 1 we move from chaos to creation, with God enthroned as the Sabbath King on day 7. In the book of Judges, however, we move backward from creation (God's people in God's land) to chaos, when "in those days there was no king in Israel" (Judg. 17:6, etc.). In other words, the structure of the book of Judges is designed to portray the "un-creation" of Israel in their rejection of the Lord as their true King. This is one way in which the book of

Judges prepares us for the events recorded in 1 Samuel, where "the LORD said to Samuel, 'Obey the voice of the people in all that they say to you, for they have not rejected you, but they have rejected me from being king over them'" (1 Sam. 8:7).

The Big Picture

Othniel teaches us that our sin stems from gospel amnesia, and Ehud teaches us that our sin is vile and disgusting. Now Deborah and Barak, Jael and Sisera teach us that our sin is ancient and evil, yet God's promises to destroy sin and evil (Gen. 3:15) still hold true, both in the dark days of the judges and in our current day.

Reflection and Discussion

Read through Judges 4:1–5:31, then engage this section of Scripture with the questions below. (For further background, see the *ESV Study Bible*, pages 444–448; available online at www.esv.org.)

1. Deborah, the Call of Barak, and the Road *from* Glory (4:1–10)

How long did Israel serve Cushan-rishathaim before the Lord raised up Othniel to deliver his people (3:8)? How long did Israel serve Eglon before the Lord raised up Ehud to deliver his people (3:14)? How long does the cruel oppression of Jabin last before the Lord raises up Deborah and Barak (4:3)? What do these numbers teach us about Israel's sin and their willingness to repent and cry out to the Lord? What does this teach us about the power of sin in our own lives and the importance of confession and repentance?

Deborah is both a judge and a prophetess—another double! How is her role as judge different from those of Othniel and Ehud?

The prophetic call of Barak by Deborah is met with an ultimatum from Barak: "If you will go with me, I will go, but if you will not go with me, I will not go" (4:8). Some have argued that this demand by Barak represents a lack of faith, but Hebrews 11:32–33 states that Barak "through faith conquered kingdoms." How can Barak's request and Deborah's response in verse 10 be understood positively? (See 2 Cor. 12:7–10.)

2. The Defeat of Sisera's Chariot Army (4:12–16)

According to Judges 4:15, who actually defeats the chariot army of Sisera?

How does the song of Judges 5 describe the battle and the defeat of the army of Sisera? See especially verses 4–5 and 20–22. Does the defeat of Sisera's chariot army in a great flood remind you of any previous battles in the life of Israel? See the Whole-Bible Connections below.

3. Sisera and Jael: Nailed It! (4:11, 17–22)

Deborah the prophetess was correct (Judg. 4:9). The defeat of Sisera comes by the hand of a woman, not by Barak. It is interesting to observe that the execution of Sisera by Jael occupies almost 30 percent of the entire narrative account

(7 of 24 verses). In light of Judges 7:2, why would the Lord choose to work in such an unexpected and unconventional way?

How does the song of Judges 5 (vv. 24–27) portray the role Jael plays in the defeat of the enemy of God's people, positively or negatively?

Why do you think so much attention is given to the gruesome way in which Jael executes Sisera? Compare Judges 4:21 and 5:26–27. See the Whole-Bible Connections below.

4. The Song of Deborah and Barak (5:1–31)

The song of Judges 5 memorializes the Lord's miraculous deliverance of Israel through Deborah (vv. 7, 12, 15), Barak (vv. 12, 15), and Jael (vv. 24–27). What does this song teach us about the events of Judges 4?

Read Exodus 15:1–21, the song of the defeat of Egypt in the Red Sea. What connections do you observe between these two songs in terms of the events described or the great themes about which they sing?

Read through the following three sections on *Gospel Glimpses*, *Whole-Bible Connections*, and *Theological Soundings*. Then take time to consider the *Personal Implications* these sections may have for you.

▶ Gospel Glimpses

STRENGTH IN WEAKNESS. It is difficult for many of us to imagine the actual terrors of the battlefield, especially when "outgunned." But just try and imagine what it would have been like for an army of Israelite farmers, poorly armed (Judg. 5:8: "Was shield or spear to be seen among forty thousand in Israel?"), to go up against an army of trained soldiers with 900 iron chariots. Victory would have seemed impossible. But this is exactly the point. God's salvation of his people is never accomplished by means of human strength but rather by the strength of God through human weakness. This is how the Lord instructs Gideon later in the book: "The people with you are too many for me to give the Midianites into their hand, lest Israel boast over me, saying, 'My own hand has saved me'" (7:2). And so, when we see Jesus hanging on the cross in the ultimate act of salvation, we see the perfection of saving weakness. This is proof that it is God at work to save! "[Christ] was crucified in weakness, but lives by the power of God. For we also are weak in him, but in dealing with you we will live with him by the power of God" (2 Cor. 13:4).

SISERA, THE ANTI-SAVIOR. Often we see pictures (types) of Christ and his salvation in the people or events recorded in the Old Testament. For example, David's victory over Goliath is a picture of Christ's victory over Satan. In addition to analogous pictures of Christ, we also see counterexamples. Sisera is one such negative image. In Judges 4, the Lord leads his people into battle, but Sisera abandons *his* people and flees as every last soldier is put to death. Sisera is an anti-savior! It is remarkable to remember that our Savior stood his ground

33

unto death in order that all of his people might live and return victorious from battle. And thus "in all these things we are more than conquerors through him who loved us" (Rom. 8:37).

Whole-Bible Connections

THE SALVATION OF THE LORD. Sometimes when reading the Bible, we experience something like déjà vu when one text is similar to another. For example, twice Abraham travels to Egypt because of a famine and passes his wife off as his sister (Genesis 12 and 20); several times men visit a well and find a wife (Genesis 24; 29; Exodus 2). These connections are intentional and help us to better understand the events. The same is true here with Judges 4–5. These chapters were written so that we would connect them to Exodus 14–15. In both accounts, the Lord defeats a great army consisting of horses and chariots by drowning them in floodwaters. In both accounts, the Lord goes out before his people and throws the enemy into great confusion. Both accounts begin with a narrative and conclude with a song. Moses and Miriam sing the song of Exodus 15, while Deborah and Barak sing the song of Judges 5. By working in this repetitive way, the Lord wisely teaches us how he will save us on that last day: by leading forth a great army to defeat the hordes of evil once and for all. This is just what the song of Judges 5 teaches us at its conclusion: "So [in this way] may all your enemies perish, O LORD!" (v. 31).

CRUSHING THE ENEMY'S HEAD. The Devil is in the details, literally, in this passage. It is no accident that the account of Jael's execution of Sisera occupies so much space in the narrative (Judg. 4:17–22; 5:24–27). The gruesome account of the striking, crushing, shattering, and piercing (5:26) of Sisera's head should cause us to remember one of the ancient promises of God from Genesis 3:15, that the offspring of the woman would one day deal the final blow to Satan and sin by crushing his head. In seeing this connection, we are reminded that Israel's greatest need is not salvation from foreign oppression but salvation from the sin that led to the oppression. In the same way, our greatest need is not to be rescued from the earthly, temporal consequences of our sin, but to be saved from sin itself and the curse of death that results from it. Even in the darkest days of our sin, the Lord is faithful to his promise.

Theological Soundings

LOVE YOUR ENEMY OR CRUSH HIS HEAD? We may feel tension between the Old Testament's glorification of the death of enemies and the New Testament's instruction to love, do good to, bless, and pray for our enemies (Luke 6:27–29). But this distinction is not so clear-cut. In the Old Testament, we see Abraham and the patriarchs doing good and blessing the people around them. Likewise, Solomon's kingship and kingdom is a tremendous blessing to the surrounding nations. On the other hand, there are accounts of judgment and death in the book of Revelation that make the wars recorded in Joshua and Judges seem like G-rated movie trailers. So how do we understand these differences? One good way to do so is to connect the dots of judgment. Israel's occupation of the land and the destruction of their enemies is intended to serve as an example of the final judgment of God, in which he will secure the inheritance of the new heavens and earth for his people by annihilating every hint of evil. The wars of Israel to exterminate the Canaanites are a fearful picture of the coming final judgment of God. Today, we live in days like those of the patriarchs, waiting for the coming of the kingdom in all of its fullness. Until that time, we live at peace with our enemies, praying for their conversion because we know of the judgment that is to come.

Personal Implications

Take time to reflect on the implications of Judges 4:1–5:31 for your life. How does this passage lead you to praise God, repent of sin, and trust more deeply in his gracious promises? Write down your reflections under the three headings we have considered and on the passage as a whole.

1. Gospel Glimpses

2. Whole-Bible Connections

3. Theological Soundings

4. Judges 4:1–5:31

As You Finish This Unit . . .

Take a few minutes to ask for God's help to grasp the significance of his great salvation as exemplified through Deborah, Barak, Jael, and even Sisera. Remember that "these things happened to them as an example, but they were written down for our instruction, on whom the end of the ages has come" (1 Cor. 10:11).

WEEK 5: GIDEON'S CALL AND COMMISSION

Judges 6:1–40

The Place of the Passage

As mentioned previously, the book of Judges contains two introductions, two conclusions, 12 judges (six major and six minor), and one anti-judge (Abimelech). Gideon is the fourth major judge as well as the leading judge in the second wave of narratives (Gideon, Jephthah, Samson). We will quickly observe that the accounts of these last three major judges are much longer than those of the first three major judges (Othniel, Ehud, Deborah/Barak). The narratives of Gideon begin in Judges 6 and run through the end of Judges 8. As Israel's decline into idolatry increases, the accounts of the Lord's salvation through these judges expands.

The Big Picture

The Lord raises up Gideon to deliver Israel through human weakness in order that Israel might know it is the Lord alone who saves and rules over his people. Gideon's response to Israel's attempt to make him king aptly summarizes the message of this section: "Gideon said to them, 'I will not rule over you, and my son will not rule over you; the LORD will rule over you'" (Judg. 8:23).

> ## Reflection and Discussion

Read through Judges 6:1–40, then engage this section of Scripture with the questions below. (For further background, see the *ESV Study Bible*, pages 448–451; available online at www.esv.org.)

1. Israel's Plight and a Prophet's Commentary (6:1–10)

In what way does Midian oppress Israel?

Israel responds to Midian's oppression in two ways. First, they hide in mountain caves and holes dug out of the ground (6:2), but this approach just makes Midian's oppression of Israel worse. Their second approach is much better. The people of Israel finally cry out to the Lord for help (6:6). This pattern still plays out today in the Christian life. When we fall into temptation and sin, we often hide from the one who has saved us from our sin, which makes things worse, not better. Do you recognize this pattern in your own life? In what ways?

When Israel cries out to the Lord for help, the Lord sends a prophet to *speak* before he sends a judge to *save* (6:7–10). The prophet delivers a word from the Lord that explains Israel's subjugation at the hand of Midian. What reason does the prophet give, and how does this reason relate to Deuteronomy 8?

2. Gideon's Call and Commission (6:11–16)

How is Gideon's question in verse 13, "Why then has all this happened to us?" answered by the speech of the prophet back in verses 8–10? For the reader, Gideon is asking a question that has already been answered, but that is the point.

The angel of the Lord commissions Gideon to save Israel from the hand of Midian "in this might of yours" (v. 14), but Gideon objects by confessing his own personal weakness and inability. Given the context of Gideon's call, what is the "might" or "strength" about which the Lord is speaking (vv. 12 and 16; see also 2:18)?

How does the "might" or "strength" of Gideon identified in verses 12 and 16 relate to the Christian life as expressed in the Great Commission: "Go therefore and make disciples of all nations, baptizing them in the name of the Father and of the Son and of the Holy Spirit, teaching them to observe all that I have commanded you. And behold, I am with you always, to the end of the age" (Matt. 28:19–20)?

3. Private and Public Songs of God's Grace (6:17–40)

Gideon asks for a private sign to confirm the identity of the angel of the Lord (v. 17). How does Gideon respond after the sign is enacted (vv. 19–21), and what truth does this sign confirm for him (v. 22)?

Seeing the angel of the Lord changes Gideon's life. Read Genesis 32:30; Exodus 33:9–11; Numbers 14:14; and Deuteronomy 34:10. Why would an experience like this have such a dramatic impact on Gideon's life? Now read 2 Corinthians 4:6 and answer the same question for your own life.

Gideon is first called to eradicate the idols in the household of his father, and he clearly obeys this command of the Lord (v. 27). The text is also clear that Gideon is "afraid" to obey such a command, given the danger of the situation. Fear and faith are not at odds, however. Gideon obeys in fear *and* by faith. When have you been truly afraid to obey the word of the Lord because you knew that it would have difficult or negative consequences in your life?

Having first destroyed the idols in the household of his father, Gideon is now called to destroy the Midianites (et al.) from the land. After summoning warriors from the tribes of Israel (vv. 34–35), Gideon asks for a public sign from the Lord—the well-known fleece signs. Many have suggested that Gideon's request shows weakness and lack of faith. But consider the facts: first, Gideon is "clothed" with the Spirit when he makes this request (v. 34); and, second, the

Lord willingly performs these signs without any rebuke of Gideon. If Gideon already knows the will of God, why does he ask the Lord to perform these fleece signs? For help, see Exodus 4:1–8.

Read through the following three sections on *Gospel Glimpses*, *Whole-Bible Connections*, and *Theological Soundings*. Then take time to consider the *Personal Implications* these sections may have for you.

Gospel Glimpses

I WILL BE WITH YOU. When Gideon needs to know how it would ever be possible for him to do the will of God in his life, the Lord answers, "I will be with you" (Judg. 6:16). When the Lord called Moses to save Israel from Egypt, Moses asked the same question and received the same answer: "I will be with you" (Ex. 3:11–12). This promise from the Lord is so central to his plan of redemption that it is enshrined in his covenantal name. Just after the Lord promised that he would "be with" Moses, the Lord revealed his covenantal name, "I AM," or "I will be" (Ex. 3:14). This raises the question, "I am" or "I will be" *what?* The answer is multifaceted, but part of the answer is surely that the Lord "will be *with you*" in light of his divine promise, "I will be with you" (Ex. 3:12). This is seen also in another Hebrew name, Immanuel, which means "God with us" (see Isa. 7:14). It is no accident, then, that the name Immanuel is applied to Jesus (Matt. 1:23) as the ultimate expression of the promise, "I will be with you." The divine presence is the one reality in the universe that can satisfy fully for all times (Ps. 16:11), and this is why it is the very hope of eternity (Rev. 21:3). The power to do the will of God is forever fueled by the promise of God in Christ, "And behold, *I am with you always*, to the end of the age" (Matt. 28:20).

YOU HAVE NOT OBEYED MY VOICE. One thing is crystal clear in the book of Judges: Israel's suffering and hardship is not due to the Lord's failure to protect and provide for his people but is due to their disobedience to God and his covenantal word (see Judg. 2:2; 6:10). This reality is as old as sin itself. The first man, Adam, experienced the same reality. Remember what God said to Adam: "Because you have listened to the voice of your wife and have eaten of the tree of which I commanded you, 'You shall not eat of it,' cursed is the ground because of you; in pain you shall eat of it all the days of your life" (Gen. 3:17). If Adam's disobedience merited God's curse, and if Israel's disobedience merited God's curse, and if we have all sinned and fallen short of the glory of God (Rom. 3:23), then what hope is there for us? The good news of the gospel is that our only hope for perfect and complete obedience from the heart is found in the obedience of Jesus Christ. Only by being united to him can we know for certain that we have God's favor. Praise God, then, that he has provided in Jesus all that he requires from us: "As by the one man's [Adam's] disobedience the many were made sinners, so by the one man's [Jesus'] obedience the many will be made righteous" (Rom. 5:19).

Whole-Bible Connections

GIDEON AND MOSES. When Gideon is called for service by the angel of the Lord, he asks about all of the great miracles performed by God in the days of Moses (Judg. 6:13). To most of us it seems as if the angel of the Lord simply ignores his question and moves forward with Gideon's commissioning, but not so. The details of the text provide the answer to Gideon's question. Since Gideon longs for the days of Moses, the Lord will make Gideon into a new Moses. The connections between Gideon and Moses are no accident; they constitute the answer to his question. Both men are called to deliver God's people from foreign oppression. Both men object by stating that they are not qualified for the job. Both men receive the promise of the divine presence as the answer to their objection. Both men receive private and public signs to confirm their calling. Both men destroy the illicit idols present in the midst of God's people. Both men build altars and make offerings to the Lord. Finally, both men speak with God face to face. When man needs a new deliverer, he needs a new Moses. When we need saving, we need a new exodus. It is no accident, then, that when the greatest act of salvation in the history of the world is to occur through Jesus, Moses reappears to speak with Jesus about his "departure," or, more precisely in Greek, his *exodus* (Luke 9:30–31).

Theological Soundings

THE WILL OF GOD. It is often thought that Gideon's fleece sign is intended to help him know the will of God for his life. As such, many modern-day

Christians ask for similar signs so that they too might know the will of God for their lives. Gideon's fleece, however, is not designed to determine the will of God for his life. On the contrary, Gideon is clear concerning God's specific will for his life. Two times, in verses 37 and 39 of Judges 6, Gideon indicates that this fleece is being offered *as a response to* the clear communication of God's will, not in order to discover it. Because Gideon is imitating Moses with these signs, we know that one purpose is to make known to Israel that the Lord has indeed appeared to Gideon and that he will deliver them through Gideon (compare Ex. 4:5). Thus, the purpose of the sign is to help God's people *do* his revealed will, not merely to help them discover it. The same is true for the Christian life today. When it comes to the will of God for his people, there is no guesswork, only homework. It is God's will for us that we should be sanctified (1 Thess. 4:3). It is God's will for us that we should "rejoice always, pray without ceasing," and "give thanks in all circumstances" (1 Thess. 5:16–18). It is God's will that we should love our enemies, forgive those who wrong us, and be generous with our resources. Jesus told us that "whoever does the will of God" is his very "brother, sister, and mother" (Mark 3:31–35), and the apostle John wrote that "whoever does the will of God abides forever" (1 John 2:17). When we pray, it is "thy will be done." It is easy to know the will of God. It is hard to do it. So what sign do we have to help us do the will of God? We have the sign of the cross (what we deserve because of our sin) and the resurrection (what we receive because of God's grace). But the fleece of the cross does not simply encourage obedience to God's will. It *is* the ultimate act of obedience to God's will, applied to us forever—something Gideon's fleece or Moses' signs could never do.

Personal Implications

Take time to reflect on the implications of Judges 6:1–40 for your life. How does this passage lead you to praise God, repent of sin, and trust more deeply in his gracious promises? Write down your reflections under the three headings we have considered and on the passage as a whole.

1. Gospel Glimpses

2. Whole-Bible Connections

3. Theological Soundings

4. Judges 6:1–40

> ### As You Finish This Unit . . .

Take a few minutes to ask for God's help to grasp the significance of his work through the call, commission, and confirmation of Gideon to deliver God's people from the sin of idolatry and the oppression of the enemy.

WEEK 6: GIDEON'S VICTORY AND DEFEAT

Judges 7:1–8:28

▲

The Place of the Passage

As mentioned previously, the book of Judges contains two introductions, two conclusions, 12 judges (six major and six minor), and one anti-judge (Abimelech). Gideon is the fourth major judge in the book of Judges, and now it is time to see the Lord work salvation for Israel *through* Gideon. Having seen Gideon called and commissioned in Judges 6, we now encounter the Lord's deliverance of Israel from Midianite oppression (7:1–25) and Israel's confusion about that deliverance (8:1–28). As we move through the accounts of the judges, Israel's sin and idolatry become progressively worse. They are now becoming blind to God's grace even as they encounter his mighty power to save.

The Big Picture

When God saves, he is careful to make clear that he has done for us what we could not do for ourselves. When we are weak, he is strong. When we come to know in the core of our being that God alone is our refuge and strength, our fear is turned into worship and the idols in our lives can finally be dislodged from our hearts.

> ## Reflection and Discussion

Read through Judges 7:1–8:28, then engage this section of Scripture with the questions below. (For further background, see the *ESV Study Bible*, pages 451–454; available online at www.esv.org.)

1. The Lord Saves Israel through Gideon and 300 Warriors (7:1–25)

Why does the Lord command Gideon to reduce the size of the army from 32,000 to 300 men (see vv. 2 and 7)?

What weapons does Gideon's army of 300 warriors use to defeat the Midianite army?

Because Gideon has only 300 warriors and a questionable weapons cache, the Lord mercifully recognizes that Gideon may have some lingering doubts about the potential success of his mission. What is Gideon's emotional condition at this time (v. 10), and how does the Lord help him (v. 11)? What is Gideon's response to the Lord's encouragement (v. 15)?

How do the 300 warriors of Israel fight the battle (see especially v. 21a)? According to verse 22, who is the real warrior of Israel, and what does he do?

2. Israel Struggles to Understand God's Saving Grace (8:1–28)

Why are the Ephraimites upset with Gideon, and how does he assuage their anger?

Some of the Israelites become upset with Gideon because they were not invited to the battle. Others, however, did not want to participate at all. Gideon cannot seem to catch a break! How do the cities of Succoth and Penuel respond to Gideon's request for help? Why is their subsequent judgment so severe?

What do the Israelites want to do for Gideon after the Lord saves Israel through him (v. 22)? Why is this offer misguided, especially in light of the statement "for you [Gideon] have saved us from the hand of Midian"? How does Gideon respond in verse 23?

What Gideon does in verses 24–27 is reminiscent of Aaron's actions in Exodus 32:1–4. How do these two accounts correspond, and what is the outcome or result of each?

Read through the following three sections on *Gospel Glimpses*, *Whole-Bible Connections*, and *Theological Soundings*. Then take time to consider the *Personal Implications* these sections may have for you.

Gospel Glimpses

FROM FEAR TO WORSHIP. Consider the kindness of God to Gideon in Judges 7:9–15. God, the true Warrior of Israel, the Creator of heaven and earth, the Judge of all nations, infinite in being, almighty in power, says in effect, "I know this plan seems crazy, and you are probably genuinely afraid, so go down to the camp of Midian and I will provide you with the encouragement that you need." God cares about his people, even about how they feel. On that day, God turns Gideon's fear into worship by assuring him of victory through a dream and its interpretation. If we are like Gideon and long for our fear to be turned into worship, we may turn to God for help. He has given us more than a dream about victory; he has given us the full assurance of victory through the bodily resurrection of Jesus Christ. Therefore, "blessed be the God and Father of our Lord Jesus Christ! According to his great mercy, he has caused us to be born again to a living hope through the resurrection of Jesus Christ from the dead" (1 Pet. 1:3; compare John 14:27).

STRENGTH IN WEAKNESS. When it comes to the plan of redemption, God is always upsetting the apple cart of human expectations. He works with Isaac, not Ishmael; Jacob, not Esau; Joseph, not Reuben. When he appoints a prophet to lead his people, he picks a man like Moses, who has trouble speaking. When he appoints a king to rule over his people, he selects the youngest brother, David, not the oldest and most experienced. When he wants to save his people from the Midianites, he selects a savior who is from the weakest of clans and is the least in his household (Judg. 6:15), commanding him to fight with only 300 torch-carrying, pot-breaking, trumpet-blowing warriors. Why would God do this? Why does he prefer to save through human weakness? So that we might know—really know—and trust, deep down, that the only one who can save God's people, either in everyday life or from eternal death, is God himself (see Isa. 43:11, 13). So, when we see the ultimate expression of human weakness hanging on the cross for our sin, we at the same time see the ultimate manifestation of God's power for the salvation of his people.

Whole-Bible Connections

THE WARRIOR OF ISRAEL. Many impressive warriors appear on the pages of the Bible. For example, Shamgar kills 600 Philistines with a cattle prod (Judg. 3:31), and Samson kills a thousand with the jawbone of a donkey (Judg. 15:15). The refrain in the book of Samuel is that "Saul has struck down his thousands, and David his ten thousands" (1 Sam. 18:7). But these pale in comparison to the true Warrior of Israel, the Lord himself. The truth that God himself fights for his people stretches across the Bible from Exodus to Revelation. We see this when the Lord delivers Israel from Egypt: "The LORD is a man of war; the LORD is his name" (Ex. 15:3; compare 15:3–16). This same reality will mark the end of the ages: "I saw heaven opened, and behold, a white horse! The one sitting on it is called Faithful and True, and in righteousness *he judges and makes war*" (Rev. 19:11; compare 19:11–16). When we encounter the Lord fighting for his people in the book of Judges (see Judg. 7:22), we are moved to confess, "Who is like you, O LORD, among the gods? Who is like you, majestic in holiness, awesome in glorious deeds, doing wonders?" (Ex. 15:11).

Theological Soundings

BOASTING. When the Lord saves through human weakness, he does so in order that we might "boast" in him and not in our own strength (Judg. 7:2). The Lord expounds on this important truth through Jeremiah the prophet: "Let not the wise man boast in his wisdom, let not the mighty man boast in his might, let not the rich man boast in his riches, but let him who boasts boast in this, that he understands and knows me, that I am the LORD who practices steadfast love, justice, and righteousness in the earth. For in these things I delight" (Jer. 9:23–24). The important theme of boasting in the Lord runs throughout Scripture. It is especially important in Paul's second letter to the Corinthians, where he concludes by stating, "But [God] said to me, 'My grace is sufficient for you, for my power is made perfect in weakness.' Therefore I will boast all the more gladly of my weaknesses, so that the power of Christ may rest upon me" (2 Cor. 12:9).

Personal Implications

Take time to reflect on the implications of Judges 7:1–8:28 for your life. How does this passage lead you to praise God, repent of sin, and trust more deeply in his gracious promises? Write down your reflections under the three headings we have considered and on the passage as a whole.

1. Gospel Glimpses

2. Whole-Bible Connections

3. Theological Soundings

4. Judges 7:1–8:28

As You Finish This Unit . . .

Take a few minutes to ask for God's help to change your fear into worship as you encounter the strength of the Warrior of Israel, the one in whom we boast, working through our weakness in order that Christ's power may rest on us.

WEEK 7: ABIMELECH, THE ANTI-JUDGE

Judges 8:29–9:57

▲

As mentioned previously, the book of Judges contains two introductions, two conclusions, 12 judges (six major and six minor), and one anti-judge (Abimelech). The nation of Israel remains "stiff-necked" and hard-hearted (Ex. 32:9; Deut. 31:27) when it comes to responding to the grace of God's saving work. With the passing of each judge, Israel falls further and further into the sin of idolatry: "As soon as Gideon died, the people of Israel turned again and whored after the Baals and made Baal-berith their god" (Judg. 8:33). This time, however, the Lord raised up not a judge to save but an "anti-judge," who would make himself king. Abimelech does not deliver Israel from foreign oppression but rather oppresses Israel from within (9:56). He is not a man possessed by the Spirit of God but rather is tormented by an evil spirit sent from God (9:23). This time, God's judgment on Israel is to give them exactly what they want.

The Big Picture

In the account of Abimelech, we see the horror of God's "yes." That is to say, God finally lets his people have exactly what they want: a king to rule over them.

53

Abimelech as king represents the rejection of the Lord as King (see 1 Sam. 10:19) and sets before our eyes the deadly curse of power and authority on our own terms (see Gen. 3:16).

> ## Reflection and Discussion

Read through Judges 8:29–9:57, then engage this section of Scripture with the questions below. (For further background, see the *ESV Study Bible*, pages 454–456; available online at www.esv.org.)

1. Abimelech's Broken Family (8:29–35)

When Gideon dies, he dies as did Abraham (Gen. 25:8) and David (1 Chron. 29:28): at "a good old age." How does the account of Gideon's death in Judges 8:32 compare with the account of Abimelech's death in 9:53–56? What does this comparison teach us?

Who is Abimelech's mother, and in what family context does Abimelech grow up? How do these factors play out in the subsequent narrative?

Israel's idolatry leads to rejection of the Lord (Judg. 8:34) and mistreatment of his people (v. 35). How do these two realities correspond to the greatest, or most important, commandment as identified by Jesus in Mark 12:29–31? Note that there is an important relationship between God and those created in his image, a relationship that is corrupted by false worship.

2. Abimelech's Broken Plan (9:1–22)

How does Abimelech convince the men of Shechem to make him king? What does it cost the men of Shechem? What does it cost the sons of Gideon?

When Jotham speaks his parable against Abimelech, atop what mountain does he stand (v. 7)? What is the significance of this mountain (see Deut. 11:29; 27:12; Josh. 8:33), and how does this reality play into the narrative of Abimelech?

In Jotham's parable, Abimelech is characterized as a "bramble" or "thorn bush." How was this imagery significant in earlier parts of Judges (see 2:3; 8:7, 16; compare Gen. 3:18), and what does it teach us about Abimelech?

3. Abimelech's Broken Skull (9:23–57)

In the final section of the Abimelech narrative, it is important to observe that God is mentioned only at the beginning (v. 23) and the end (vv. 56–57). Though it may seem that God is silent in this section of the narrative, he is not absent. How do we see God's working in this narrative as he gives Israel over to their sinful desires? What is God's purpose in allowing the events to unfold in this way?

How do those who worship Baal-berith in Shechem die (vv. 46–49)? How is this form of judgment ironic and suited to the sin of idolatry?

How does Abimelech die (vv. 53–54), and in what way is his death similar to that of Sisera earlier in Judges (4:21)? Given all the possible ways in which the Lord could have orchestrated the death of Abimelech, what is the possible significance of this particular type of death (compare Gen. 3:15 and Matt. 27:33)?

Read through the following three sections on *Gospel Glimpses*, *Whole-Bible Connections*, and *Theological Soundings*. Then take time to consider the *Personal Implications* these sections may have for you.

▶ Gospel Glimpses

REMEMBERING THE GOSPEL. Israel's unfaithfulness is, once again, due to gospel amnesia. In Judges 8:34 we read, "The people of Israel *did not remember* the LORD their God, who had delivered them from the hand of all their enemies on every side." Because of the nature of our hearts, it is easy to forget that God is the one who truly saves, sustains, and grows us—both in this life and in the next. We need weekly, daily, and even hourly reminders of God's saving gospel grace. The dark horror of the Abimelech narrative reminds us of the deadly consequences of neglecting the good news of the gospel as fuel for the obedience of faith. So, then, we must "remember Jesus Christ, risen from the dead, the offspring of David, as preached in my gospel" (2 Tim. 2:8).

▶ Whole-Bible Connections

KINGSHIP. An important theme in the book of Judges is that of kingship, a theme intended to prepare readers for encountering the Davidic monarchy in 1 Samuel. In Judges 1, we witness the lengthy success of the tribe of Judah (the tribe of David) and the brief failure of the tribe of Benjamin (the tribe of Saul). When Gideon delivers Israel from the Midianites, they want to make him their ruler, but he rightly responds, "I will not rule over you, and *my son* will not rule over you; *the LORD will rule over you*" (Judg. 8:23). It is ironic, then, that the men of Shechem make Abimelech, *Gideon's son,* king over them. At the end of the book of Judges, we encounter the reason for Israel's pathetic condition: "In those days there was no king in Israel. [And so] everyone did what was right in his own eyes" (21:25; compare 17:6; 18:1; 19:1). But we miss the point if we think that the author is referring only to human kingship. Israel's desire for a king represents their rejection of the Lord as King, as Samuel will later explain: "Today you have rejected your God, who saves you from all your calamities and your distresses, and you have said to him, 'Set a king over us'" (1 Sam. 10:19). When we want "the thing" more than we want the one who provides it, we have fallen prone to the corrupting core of idolatry.

LOVE YOUR NEIGHBOR. Some readers are surprised to discover that the command to love one's neighbor is as old as Leviticus 19:18: "You shall not take vengeance or bear a grudge against the sons of your own people, but you shall *love your neighbor* as yourself." Of course, we are familiar with this command because Jesus designated it one of the greatest or most important of the commandments (Matt. 22:39; Mark 12:31; Luke 10:27). Even in the Decalogue (the Ten Commandments), more than half of the individual commands fall under the heading of "love your neighbor." In the book of Judges, we learn that the rejection of God (Judg. 8:34) corrupts the relationships we share with one another. For instance, Israel's idolatrous rejection of the Lord results in horrific mistreatment of Gideon's family (8:35). False worship always corrupts the relationship between God and those created in his image.

Theological Soundings

AN EVIL SPIRIT. The Lord is sovereign over both the visible and the invisible kingdoms of reality. We know that he constrains and commands even Satan on our behalf (see Job 1). When the Lord sends an evil spirit between Abimelech and the people of Shechem, he begins the process of bringing judgment on these two offending parties. The same thing will happen to Saul. After David is anointed king, the Lord sends an evil spirit to torment Saul and so destroy his kingship (1 Sam. 16:14). In the Gospels, we see Jesus' complete authority over the evil spirits as they obey his every word. Spirits of this type are not free to run wild and wreak havoc without any constraint. From beginning to end, we see God's gracious power to constrain and subjugate such evil.

SIN AND ITS CONSEQUENCES. One of the real terrors of sin, especially idolatry such as that practiced in the book of Judges, is that it contains "built-in" judgment: "Those who make [idols] become like them; so do all who trust in them" (Ps. 115:8). What does Abimelech's kingship bring? It brings death—death to his family and death to the people over whom he reigned. Israel wanted to worship Baal-berith, but what is their fate? They are consumed in the tower of Baal-berith, like the very sacrifices they offered to that false god. Those who trust in idols become like the idols they serve and so are "receiving in themselves the due penalty for their error" (Rom. 1:27; compare 1:26–32).

Personal Implications

Take time to reflect on the implications of Judges 8:29–9:57 for your life. How does this passage lead you to praise God, repent of sin, and trust more deeply in his gracious promises? Write down your reflections under the three headings we have considered and on the passage as a whole.

1. Gospel Glimpses

2. Whole-Bible Connections

3. Theological Soundings

4. Judges 8:29–9:57

> ### As You Finish This Unit . . .

Take a few minutes to ask for God's help as you consider the account of Abimelech, the anti-judge. Let us not fail to remember the Lord, "who will transform our lowly body to be like his glorious body, by the power that enables him even to subject all things to himself" (Phil. 3:21).

WEEK 8: JEPHTHAH AND HIS ONLY BEGOTTEN

Judges 10:1–12:15

▲

The Place of the Passage

As mentioned previously, the book of Judges contains two introductions, two conclusions, 12 judges (six major and six minor), and one anti-judge (Abimelech). In the three short chapters forming this week's study, we encounter six of the 12 total judges in the book of Judges. Jephthah is the fifth major judge in the book (10:6–12:7) and he is flanked by two minor judges at the beginning of this section, Tola (10:1–2) and Jair (10:3–5), and by three minor judges at the end—Ibzon (12:8–10), Elon (12:11–12), and Abdon (12:13–15). It is difficult to know exactly why there is such a concentration of judges in this section of the book, although it likely serves, among other purposes, to focus our attention on the accounts of the final two major judges in the book, Jephthah and Samson. As Israel continues to fall more and more into sin and idolatry, her oppression by the enemy also increases. As Israel's sin and oppression increase, so does the cost of deliverance for the judge. For Jephthah, Israel's deliverance costs him his only child.

The Big Picture

The Lord calls Jephthah, the outcast son of a prostitute, to deliver Israel from the oppression of the Ammonites. This deliverance costs him his only daughter and also results in national strife by which Israel is torn apart from within.

> **Reflection and Discussion**

Read through Judges 10:1–12:15, then engage this section of Scripture with the questions below. (For further background, see the *ESV Study Bible*, pages 457–460; available online at www.esv.org.)

1. Encountering the Minor Judges (10:1–5; 12:8–15)

The five minor judges that appear in this section are presented to us in a framework or structure that includes (1) the judge's name; (2) his family or place of origin; (3) his years of service as judge; and, finally, (4) his death and burial account. Can you identify all four parts in each of the narratives of the five minor judges?

The narratives of three of the minor judges in this section include additional information concerning sons, daughters, grandsons, marriage, donkeys, and/ or cities. What does this information tell us about the judges and their families at this time in the history of Israel?

2. Israel's Sin and the Lord's Faithfulness (10:6–18)

Israel's idolatry is out of control; how many gods or sets of gods are they now serving in their rejection of the Lord (see v. 6)? Israel's sin is matched only by the Lord's gracious salvation. From how many nations has the Lord delivered his people (see vv. 11–12)? How do these realities of idolatry and deliverance correspond to Joshua 21:43–45 and 23:1–16?

In the judge cycles, Israel does evil; the Lord becomes angry; he gives Israel into the hand of oppressors; and then Israel cries out to God for help. At this point in the present cycle, we would expect the Lord to raise up a judge to deliver his people. In this case, however, the Lord responds differently. How does the Lord respond to Israel's cry for help? How is the Lord's response ultimately a gracious response?

3. The Lord Delivers Israel through Jephthah (11:1–33)

Describe Jephthah's family situation. Why would this make him an unexpected or unqualified savior in the eyes of Israel? Can you think of other such unexpected deliverers in the Bible? Why do you think the Lord often works in this way?

What is Jephthah's first approach in dealing with the enemy: war, or covenantal diplomacy? What is the ultimate basis for his approach, as described in verse 27?

What does this say about the character of Jephthah, especially as he is presented in 1 Samuel 12:11 and Hebrews 11:32ff.?

---

4. Jephthah's (In)famous Vow (11:30–31, 34–40)

What is the vow that Jephthah promises to fulfill if the Lord will deliver Israel through him? Is this a wise or unwise vow? Why?

Jephthah makes his vow while in a particular spiritual condition (see v. 29). How does Jephthah's "condition" shape how we should think about his vow?

How is the fulfillment and impact of Jephthah's vow described in verses 39–40? Why do you think the fulfillment of the vow is described in this way?

---

5. Israel's Response to God's Gracious Salvation (12:1–15)

How does the tribe of Ephraim respond to the Lord's gracious salvation? What does this teach us about the true terror of idolatry in Israel? What makes it so difficult at times for us to see the Lord's grace presented in the Scriptures and yet not respond with repentance and worship?

Read through the following three sections on *Gospel Glimpses, Whole-Bible Connections*, and *Theological Soundings*. Then take time to consider the *Personal Implications* these sections may have for you.

▶ Gospel Glimpses

THE MERCY OF THE LORD'S IMPATIENCE. Israel's reoccurring idolatry is like an unfaithful wife who repeatedly whores after other men while forsaking a faithful and forgiving husband. The Lord is finally weary of Israel's unfaithfulness, and so he gives his people into the hands of those they have loved and worshiped: "I will save you no more. Go and cry out to the gods whom you have chosen; let them save you in the time of your distress" (Judg. 10:13–14). This, however, is not the end of the story. Israel's self-inflicted misery and oppression quickly provokes the Lord to action when "he became impatient over the misery of Israel" (10:16). Yes, the Lord is slow to anger, but he is also quick to save when his people repent, like a loving husband who longs for the return of his beloved wife. This is why the Lord states, "Those whom I love, I reprove and discipline, so be zealous and repent" (Rev. 3:19).

HIS ONLY CHILD. Pictures of the gospel in the book of Judges often appear hidden to us. However, gospel realities live on every page. The judges were men and women of faith (Heb. 11:32–33) whose lives point forward to the person and work of Jesus (John 5:39) and constitute the gospel promised beforehand (Rom. 1:1–3). Remember that Jephthah's vow in Judges 11:30 was made under the influence of the Spirit of God, as recorded for us in the previous verse (v. 29). Jephthah's saving of God's people cost him "his only child" (v. 34). In the Old Testament, this designation is applied to only one other person: Isaac, in God's command to Abraham to "take your son, your only son Isaac, whom you love, and go to the land of Moriah, and offer him there as a burnt offering on one of the mountains of which I shall tell you" (Gen. 22:2). We often say that salvation is God's "free gift" to those who believe. It is free, however, only because someone else paid the price, the price of his only Child. Scripture teaches us that God loved the world in this way: "He gave his only Son, that whoever believes in him should not perish but have eternal life" (John 3:16).

Whole-Bible Connections

MAKING SACRIFICES TO THE LORD. In Judges 11:31, Jephthah vows to offer as a "burnt offering" whatever comes out of his house to meet him, when and if he returns victorious from battle. It is important to understand that in both the Old and New Testaments, literal sacrifices and offerings could be used symbolically. For example, in Exodus 29 and Leviticus 8, Aaron and his sons (the Levites) are symbolically offered to the Lord as a wave offering (an offering typically consumed completely with fire) in a gesture of complete and total dedication to the Lord's service. In Psalm 51:17, a broken and contrite heart is the sacrifice the Lord desires. And in Romans 12:1, Paul admonished believers to offer their bodies as living sacrifices to the Lord as an act of spiritual worship. Thus it is possible that Jephthah, under the Spirit's guidance, uses the language of sacrifice symbolically when he offers his only daughter to the Lord.

THE SACRIFICE OF SERVICE. Child sacrifice is clearly a forbidden abomination in Scripture (Deut. 12:31; 18:9–12; compare 2 Kings 3:27; 23:10; Isa. 57:5). The bigger concern in our text, however, is not of death but of virginity. In Judges 11:37, Jephthah's daughter requests a two-month leave in order to lament her virginity. In verse 38, the text records that, while accompanied by her friends, Jephthah's daughter weeps about her virginity. Then, in verse 39, it is recorded that Jephthah fulfills his vow to the Lord, and the text describes an implication of this vow: "She had never known a man." It is possible, therefore, that Jephthah's vow consists of offering a member of his house to the full-time service of the Lord and thus not to the typical duties of a household, such as marriage and childbearing. Service of this type is not unknown in the Old Testament (Ex. 38:8; 1 Sam. 2:22; compare 1 Sam. 1:11, 22–28), and the apostle Paul testifies to its value in the New Testament as well (1 Cor. 7:7–8).

Theological Soundings

MAKING VOWS. Making vows or promises, especially to the Lord, is a serious matter. He has explained in his Word, "If you make a vow to the LORD your God, you shall not delay fulfilling it, for the LORD your God will surely require it of you, and you will be guilty of sin. But if you refrain from vowing, you will not be guilty of sin. You shall be careful to do what has passed your lips, for you have voluntarily vowed to the LORD your God what you have promised with your mouth" (Deut. 23:21–23). This same reality holds true in the New Testament (Matt. 5:37). Believers must be exceedingly careful in making vows and must be wholeheartedly intent on fulfilling them. To break a vow before the Lord has serious consequences, even if they are not immediately visible.

ATONEMENT FOR SIN. We are reminded by the extreme cost of Jephthah's vow, and its connection to the binding of Isaac, that "it is impossible for the blood of bulls and goats to take away sins" (Heb. 10:4). The sacrifices of the Old Testament remind us about the cost required to pay for our sin. But the fact that the Levitical sacrifices for sin had to be offered continuously is evidence that animal sacrifices never were meant to pay the price of sin. They pointed beyond themselves to something greater, since "we have been sanctified through the offering of the body of Jesus Christ once for all" (Heb. 10:10).

Personal Implications

Take time to reflect on the implications of Judges 10:1–12:15 for your life. How does this passage lead you to praise God, repent of sin, and trust more deeply in his gracious promises? Write down your reflections under the three headings we have considered and on the passage as a whole.

1. Gospel Glimpses

2. Whole-Bible Connections

3. Theological Soundings

4. Judges 10:1–12:15

> ### As You Finish This Unit . . .

Take a few minutes to ask for God's help to grasp the significance of his "impatience to save" and the cost of that salvation as we encounter the sacrifice of Jephthah's only child. What a great salvation the people of God possess! God has expressed the measure of his love for us in the cost he was willing to pay to redeem us.

WEEK 9: SAMSON IN TIMNAH

Judges 13:1–15:20

As mentioned previously, the book of Judges contains two introductions, two conclusions, 12 judges (six major and six minor), and one anti-judge (Abimelech). Samson is the climactic judge in the book of Judges. The account of his service is divided into two parts, chapters 13–15 and chapter 16, each concluding with a statement recording the number of years that he served as judge: "And he judged Israel in the days of the Philistines twenty years" (15:20; compare 16:31).

The Big Picture

The Lord raised up Samson to save Israel from the hand of the Philistines at great personal cost. In the first account, Samson's Spirit-empowered victories come through the betrayal of his bride and the cost of her life.

> **Reflection and Discussion**

Read through Judges 13:1–15:20, then engage this section of Scripture with the questions below. (For further background, see the *ESV Study Bible*, pages 461–465; available online at www.esv.org.)

1. The Birth of a Savior (13:1–25)

The cycle begins just as we might expect: Israel does evil in the eyes of the Lord, and so the Lord gives Israel into the hands of the enemy. This time, the Lord gives Israel into the hands of the infamous Philistines for 40 years, the longest period of oppression in the book of Judges. Given the pattern of the judge cycles, what should come next? What appears to be missing from this judge narrative? What might this omission teach us?

Among all the judges, Samson is unique. He is introduced with a lengthy birth narrative. What does this birth account teach us about the upcoming life and ministry of Samson? What type of judge will Samson be? How would you answer the question of his father, "What is to be the child's manner of life, and what is his mission?" (Judg. 13:12).

Birth narratives are rare and thus important in the Old and New Testaments. Only seven are found across the pages of Scripture. Can you identify any of the other biblical characters who are introduced by birth narratives? What do these individuals have in common?

_____

_____

_____

_____

_____

_____

The birth account of Samson in Judges 13 and the birth account of John the Baptist in Luke 1 share many common features. In fact, it appears that Luke has modeled his account of John the Baptist's birth after Samson's. Comparing Judges 13 and Luke 1, can you identify the major features they share? What does the connection between these two men through their birth accounts teach us about Samson?

_____

_____

_____

_____

_____

_____

2. Samson and His Philistine Bride (14:1–15:20)

We are often tricked into thinking that Samson's great strength is the secret to his success. But the Bible tells us something different. According to Judges 13:24–25 and 14:6, 19, what is the key component to both Samson's great strength and his success? How is the source of Samson's great strength available to us for Christian living today (see Zech. 4:6; Rom. 15:13; Eph. 3:16; 2 Tim. 1:7)?

_____

_____

_____

_____

_____

Samson's request to marry a Philistine is surprising, especially to his parents (Judg. 14:3). What do we learn from verse 4 about Samson's reason for seeking this marriage—a reason of which his parents are unaware? How does this important fact impact how we think about Samson's request and all of the terrible events that follow?

Why would the Bible be interested to tell us that Samson killed a lion under the influence of the Spirit, only to return later to eat honey from it (14:5–9)? How does this event play into the tragedy at Timnah (14:10–15:17)? How does this event connect Samson to other biblical "servants" (15:18; compare 1 Sam. 17:36–37; Matt. 3:4)?

Samson's subjugation of the Philistines in Judges 15 is unconventional. His weapons include 300 foxes, 150 torches, and the jawbone of a donkey. Why would the Lord choose to work through Samson in this way?

Who handed Samson into the hands of the Philistines? What does this say about the condition of Israel at this time? Why is the statement of Judges 15:11 so tragic: "Do you not know that the Philistines are rulers over us?"

Read through the following three sections on *Gospel Glimpses, Whole-Bible Connections,* and *Theological Soundings.* Then take time to consider the *Personal Implications* these sections may have for you.

Gospel Glimpses

I THIRST. When Samson is thirsty unto death, the Lord miraculously provides water for his servant to drink (Judg. 15:18–19). When Elijah is thirsty unto death, the Lord miraculously provides water for his servant to drink (1 Kings 19:4–18). When Jesus is thirsty unto death, the Father does *not* provide water for his *Son* to drink (John 19:28–30). Jesus is denied the water of life in order that we might drink from the everlasting well. As our Savior said of himself, "If anyone thirsts, let him come to me and drink. Whoever believes in me, as the Scripture has said, 'Out of his heart will flow rivers of living water'" (John 7:37–38).

THE BETRAYAL OF A BRIDE. Israel's idolatry is just like unfaithfulness to a marriage covenant. Israel has become the unfaithful bride of the Lord as they whore after the gods of the nations around them (see Ezekiel 16; Hosea 1–3). In Judges 14–15, the relationship between Samson and his bride is depicted much like the relationship between the Lord and Israel: betrayal, unfaithfulness, and subjugation at the hands of another husband. The account of this bride ends in the great tragedy of her death. This is what Israel deserved, and this is what we also deserve as unfaithful members of the covenant. But the Lord will not allow his people, his bride-church, to perish like the bride of Samson. "Let us rejoice and exult and give him the glory, for the marriage of the Lamb has come, and his Bride has made herself ready; it was granted her to clothe herself with fine linen, bright and pure" (Rev. 19:7–8; compare 21:2, 9).

Whole-Bible Connections

IT'S A BOY! Ever since the promise of Genesis 3:15, God's people have waited for the birth of the offspring of the woman who would crush the head of the serpent and forever deliver God's people from sin and death. This is why the Bible features seven important birth narratives that anticipate the arrival of the promised seed of the woman. The births of Isaac and Jacob showcase the miraculous nature of this birth and the faithfulness of God to keep his gospel promise. The births of Moses, Samson, Samuel, and John the Baptist remind us that God's promised seed will perform a great act of salvation for his people. It is only in the seventh and final birth narrative, however, that the miraculous

Seed-Savior arrives in the person of Jesus, who was born to save his people from their sins (Matt. 1:21).

SAMSON AND JOHN THE BAPTIST. As previously noted, Samson and John the Baptist are related in a special way—not in a family relationship but rather in a redemptive relationship. Both of their births are uniquely announced by an angel of the Lord. Both mothers were previously barren. Both men are designated as Nazirites for life and are appointed by the Lord to special service. Tragically, both men are betrayed by women unto death: Samson by Delilah (Judges 16) and John the Baptist by Herodias's daughter (Mark 6). These men serve faithfully, but their main role is to point beyond themselves to the coming of a king. For Samson that king is David, but for John the Baptist that king is the greater, promised son of David, the Lord Jesus Christ (Rom. 1:3).

Theological Soundings

ETHICS AND EXPECTATIONS. Some interpreters apply the life of Samson to believers today by teaching that if God can use someone like Samson, a terrible sinner, then he can certainly use people like us to serve in his church. Sure, they say, we are sinners, but we are certainly not as bad as Samson. In reality, however, Samson is a type of Christ, not a type of you or me. Samson and Jesus are saviors, and we are those who need saving. If we want to identity with anyone in the book of Judges, we should identify with the people of Israel—those who continue doing evil in the sight of the Lord despite his saving grace. Some readers may be shocked to discover that Samson is not portrayed as sinful in these chapters of the book of Judges. His marriage is not forbidden by the Mosaic covenant (remember Moses, Boaz, and the husband of Rahab the prostitute—although intermarriage with certain nations *was* forbidden; see Deut. 7:3), and he was born to kill Philistines. This was his special calling from the Lord, to deliver the Israelites from the Philistines, and he is successful in this calling! Tragically, the way in which we think about Samson today is much like the way in which the Pharisees thought of Jesus: associating with the wrong women, eating and healing on the Sabbath, identifying himself as God, etc. We should be careful how we judge these saviors, all the more so as we erroneously liken them to ourselves.

Personal Implications

Take time to reflect on the implications of Judges 13:1–15:20 for your life. How does this passage lead you to praise God, repent of sin, and trust more deeply in his gracious promises? Write down your reflections under the three headings we have considered and on the passage as a whole.

1. Gospel Glimpses

2. Whole-Bible Connections

3. Theological Soundings

4. Judges 13:1–15:20

As You Finish This Unit . . .

Take a few minutes to ask for God's help to grasp the great salvation of God delivered though his servant Samson, one of the men who, according to the New Testament, "through faith conquered kingdoms, enforced justice, obtained promises, stopped the mouths of lions, quenched the power of fire, escaped the edge of the sword, were made strong out of weakness, became mighty in war, [and] put foreign armies to flight" (Heb. 11:33–34).

Week 10: Samson in Gaza

Judges 16:1–31

▲

As mentioned previously, the book of Judges contains two introductions, two conclusions, 12 judges (six major judges and six minor judges), and one anti-judge (Abimelech). Samson is the climactic judge in the book of Judges. The account of his service is divided into two parts, chapters 13–15 and chapter 16, each concluding with a statement recording the number of years that he served as judge: "And he judged Israel in the days of the Philistines twenty years" (15:20; compare 16:31).

The Big Picture

The Lord raises up Samson to save Israel from the hand of the Philistines at great personal cost. In this second account, Samson's betrayal, humiliation, and death lead to his greatest act of deliverance.

> ## Reflection and Discussion

Read through Judges 16:1–31, then engage this section of Scripture with the questions below. (For further background, see the *ESV Study Bible*, pages 465–466; available online at www.esv.org.)

1. Samson and the Prostitute (16:1–3)

Gaza was one of five major Philistine cities (Josh. 13:3). Read Joshua 2:1–7 and note the parallels between the spies' trip to Jericho and Samson's trip to Gaza. Given these parallels, why would Samson have stayed with a prostitute in Gaza?

In an act of Spirit-empowered strength, Samson removes the gates of Gaza and marches them some 50 miles to Hebron. In war, the destruction of city gates is strategic because it renders a city vulnerable (see Jer. 51:30; Lam. 2:9; Amos 1:5). In this case, however, it is not just strategic. Read Genesis 22:17; 24:60, and explain how Samson's removal of the city gates is a sign of God's faithfulness to his people.

2. Samson and Delilah (16:4–31)

At birth, Samson had been designated a Nazirite for life. Read Numbers 6:1–21 and summarize the requirements of a Nazirite. What was the purpose of this special vow?

How many times does Delilah seek to discover the secret of Samson's strength (Judg. 16:4–31)? What does Samson tell her in each instance?

Samson finally tells Delilah the secret to his strength, and she betrays him by cutting his hair and breaking his Nazirite vow. What happens to Samson when his hair is cut, and what does this tell us about the true nature of his strength (see vv. 17–20)?

What do the Philistines do to Samson once they capture him? Why do they eventually bring him into the temple of Dagon, a Philistine god?

Given Samson's calling as judge to deliver Israel from Philistine oppression, how should we think about Samson's death in light of the summary statement, "So the dead whom he killed at his death were more than those whom he had killed during his life" (v. 30)?

Read through the following three sections on *Gospel Glimpses*, *Whole-Bible Connections*, and *Theological Soundings*. Then take time to consider the *Personal Implications* these sections may have for you.

Gospel Glimpses

A SUFFERING SERVANT. Some may argue that Samson is a muscle-bound, brainless Hebrew Hercules. However, he is better understood as one of Israel's suffering servants, a man who stood alone to suffer betrayal, humiliation, great physical pain, and even death in order to deliver God's people from the power of the enemy. In Mark 14:58, Jesus is accused of seeking to destroy a temple, something Samson actually does to the temple of Dagon. Jesus is betrayed by those he loves, sold for a bag of silver, blindfolded, beaten, mocked, and handed over to the enemy, just like Samson. And Jesus' death is his greatest act of deliverance, as is Samson's. The Christian gospel contains some sharp edges. The account of Samson is no sanitized form of the gospel. If we reject Samson, then we also reject the one to whom he points. And if we reject the one to whom he points, then we are tragically lost. Christ, whom Samson foreshadows, shows us the cost of bearing the curse our sin has merited: the life of the very one who had the right to bring forth our condemnation. In his death, Jesus saved many more than in his life.

WHO IS SAMSON? The Philistines captured Samson. They put out his eyes, shackled him, put him in prison, and set him to forced labor. This was all possible because Delilah put the razor to Samson's hair, violating his Nazirite vow and causing the Lord to depart from him. Why did the Lord allow this? Because by these actions Samson became the very image of Israel: blinded by idolatry, subjugated by foreigners, and forced to work and provide for the enemy through tribute. God was about to deliver Israel from this enemy, but not before teaching them about their own condition as a people. Samson had become a living lesson for the people of Israel. The horror of Samson's condition at the end of his life should remind us about the horror of sin's corruption in our own lives. Samson endured the shame of Israel's sin so that we might see clearly our need to repent and worship the one who freely endured the shame of our sin on the cross.

Whole-Bible Connections

THE GATES OF YOUR ENEMIES. Sometimes we might struggle to understand why certain things appear in the Bible. The account in Judges 16:1–3 is one such account. Samson spends the night at the house of a prostitute and, in the middle of the night, tears the city gates from the wall and takes them on a 50-mile trip.

In this account, however, God is hard at work to show us his faithfulness to keep all of his promises, even the smaller ones that we might have forgotten. Israel's possession of the gates of their enemies is an old patriarchal promise, made to Abraham in Genesis 22:17: "I will surely bless you, and I will surely multiply your offspring as the stars of heaven and as the sand that is on the seashore. *And your offspring shall possess the gate of his enemies.*" In the book of Judges, Israel had forgotten God and his promises. But God never forgets; God reminds us, even here, that he will always keep his promises. "All the promises of God find their Yes in [Jesus]. That is why it is through him that we utter our Amen to God for his glory" (2 Cor. 1:20).

Theological Soundings

BETRAYAL, SUFFERING, AND DISCIPLESHIP. We may think that Samson is foolish to reveal the source of his strength to Delilah, but the biblical text does not tell us one way or the other. We do know, however, that the two women Samson loves betray him to the enemy and, in the first case, that this "was from the LORD, for he was seeking an opportunity against the Philistines" (Judg. 14:4). The experience of betrayal and suffering is a hallmark of God's people in this world. In addition to Samson and Jesus, we are reminded of people such as Joseph, Moses, David, Daniel, and the apostle Paul. All of these are betrayed and suffer in service to the kingdom of God. Because we live in a fallen world, Christian discipleship often lives in the context of suffering and betrayal, and so we should not be surprised when we encounter suffering as we continue to wait for the consummation of all things (1 Pet. 4:12–13). As the apostle Paul reflects, "I consider that the sufferings of this present time are not worth comparing with the glory that is to be revealed to us" (Rom. 8:18). Samson understood this, and so he refused to "accept release, so that [he] might rise again to a better life" (Heb. 11:35).

Personal Implications

Take time to reflect on the implications of Judges 16:1–31 for your life. How does this passage lead you to praise God, repent of sin, and trust more deeply in his gracious promises? Write down your reflections under the three headings we have considered and on the passage as a whole.

1. Gospel Glimpses

2. Whole-Bible Connections

3. Theological Soundings

4. Judges 16:1–31

As You Finish This Unit . . .

Take a few minutes to ask for God's help to appreciate fully the Samson narratives as the gospel "promised beforehand." Consider the great price Samson paid to deliver his people temporarily from the oppression of the Philistines and how this points us forward to the one who delivered us not from the Philistines but from sin and death.

WEEK 11: EVERYONE DID WHAT WAS RIGHT IN HIS OWN EYES

Judges 17:1–21:25

▲

The Place of the Passage

As mentioned previously, the book of Judges contains two introductions, two conclusions, 12 judges (six major and six minor), and one anti-judge (Abimelech). As we come to chapter 17 we have finally arrived at the double conclusion to the book of Judges. This double conclusion is intentionally designed to mirror the double introduction in Judges 1:1–3:6. Here we discover the same two basic themes taken up by the author, but in reverse order: (1) the crisis of Israel's faith expressed through idolatry in Judges 17–18, and (2) the crisis of Israel's inheritance expressed through tribal extermination in Judges 19–21. In these final chapters, there are no more judges to lead Israel, either in battle or in faithful living.

The Big Picture

The explanation of these difficult narrative accounts is stated explicitly: "In those days there was no king in Israel. Everyone did what was right in his own eyes" (Judg. 17:6; compare 18:1; 19:1; 21:25). These final narratives illustrate life in Israel during the time of the judges, when "everyone did what was right in his own eyes." We also learn that this state of affairs was related to the fact that Israel had no king. We encounter homemade religion and do-it-yourself conquest (chs. 17–18) before watching with despair as the Israelites become Canaanites (chs. 19–21).

> ### Reflection and Discussion

Read through Judges 17–21, then engage this section of Scripture with the questions below. (For further background, see the *ESV Study Bible*, pages 467–474; available online at www.esv.org.)

1. Homemade Religion and Do-It-Yourself Conquest (chs. 17–18)

The conclusion to the book of Judges begins with the introduction of Micah, a thief and purveyor of homemade religion. How do his actions in these opening verses relate to the statement that began each of the major judge narratives: "And the people of Israel again did what was evil in the sight of the Lord" (see 2:11; 3:7, 12; 4:1; 6:1; 10:6; 13:1)?

When Micah acquires a Levite as a priest for his home shrine, he comes to the conclusion that his prosperity is guaranteed: "Now I know that the Lord will prosper me, because I have a Levite as priest" (17:13). What is the flaw in his thinking (see Deut. 29:19; Ps. 51:16–17; Isa. 66:2)? How are Christians today led astray by this same type of thinking?

Compare the way in which Israel's conquest is described in Judges 1:1–4 with the conquest of the tribe of Dan in 18:6, 10, 27–28. What is the major difference between these two accounts, and what does this teach us about the conquest of Laish?

Why does the Levite leave the house of Micah to serve the tribe of Dan (18:19–20)? What does this teach us about the character of the Levite? How can we be tempted in the same way?

The final verses in Judges 18 describe the spiritual climate and condition of the city of Dan (formerly Laish). How do these facts help us to understand the spiritual condition of Israel in a time when people chose to do what was right in their own eyes? See Deuteronomy 29:16–21.

2. Benjaminites Become Canaanites (chs. 19–21)

When returning home with his concubine, why does the Levite refuse to spend the night in Jebus (or Jerusalem)? Where do the Levite and his traveling companions finally lodge for the night? What do we know about this city from 1 Samuel 10:26?

Read Genesis 19:1–11 and compare those events with what is recorded in Judges 19:22–26. What does this tell us about the people of Benjamin living in Gibeah? See Deuteronomy 29:16–28.

How does the Levite respond to the death of his concubine? What does he do, and what action does this provoke when Israel is assembled at Mizpah? (Judg. 19:27–30).

We have come to learn in the book of Judges that it is the Lord, the Warrior of Israel, who fights for Israel against their enemies. What does it mean, then, when we encounter this statement that describes the defeat of Benjamin: "The LORD defeated Benjamin before Israel, and the people of Israel destroyed 25,100 men of Benjamin that day" (20:35)?

How do the people of Israel respond to the defeat of the tribe of Benjamin in Judges 21:3? How do they attempt to reverse this crisis, and how is this, once again, an illustration of the final words in the book, "Everyone did what was right in his own eyes" (21:25)?

Read through the following three sections on *Gospel Glimpses, Whole-Bible Connections*, and *Theological Soundings*. Then take time to consider the *Personal Implications* these sections may have for you.

Gospel Glimpses

KINGSHIP AND OBEDIENCE. Why was a lack of kingship tied to Israel's disobedience, or doing what was right in their own eyes? We always serve that which reigns as king in our lives, and this service governs how we live and think. If money is king, we serve the idol of money. If sex is our king, then we live for this idol. If power or comfort or freedom or grades in school or intellect or anything else is our idol, then we will serve that which reigns on the throne of our hearts. Our behavior is simply the manifestation of this kingship. And so, if the incarnate Word does not reign in our heart as King, then we are called to wage war and put to death the idols of false kingship in our hearts. The power to put these idols to death comes from the King who was put to death for our sin. He has come, he has conquered, and, in so doing, he has nailed our sin to the cross on which he died. Our sin is killed by our faith in Christ that rests, more and more, in his work, in his effort, in his victory. Our own best efforts will not get it done. Our best religion will not get it done. Only faith in the one who achieved victory for us, the King who came to our land, is sufficient.

Whole-Bible Connections

BENJAMIN AND SODOM. Mark Twain is reputed to have said, "History doesn't repeat itself, but it does rhyme." Judges 19 was written in such a way that it would "rhyme" with Genesis 19, the account of Lot and the two angelic visitors to the town of Sodom. There are multiple parallels between these two accounts, such as travelers arriving at night and planning to sleep in the city square; hospitality coming not from a resident but from a sojourner in the city; men of the city surrounding the house, pounding on the door, and interrupting a meal; men of the city seeking to engage in illicit sexual relations with the male visitors; a host protesting this great evil; two women offered as substitutes for the male visitors; and the inhabitants of the city destroyed by an act of judgment. But there is one major difference between the accounts: in Genesis 19, the evils of Sodom are performed by Canaanites, but in Judges 19, the evildoers are Israelites—God's people. Just as God had warned the Israelites (Deut. 7:1–6; 18:9), due to their inability or refusal to drive the Canaanites out of the land, God's people had become just like their evil neighbors.

BENJAMIN AND SAUL. The book of Judges was designed to prepare us for the arrival of the monarchy in 1 Samuel. On four occasions in these final chapters the author declares, "There was no king in Israel." Another way in which the book of Judges prepares us for the coming monarchy is by its characterization of the tribe of Benjamin. Recall in Judges 1 that Benjamin's occupation of the land was described as a failure, allowing the Canaanites to live among them (Judg. 1:21). Now, at the end of the book, we see that the tribe of Benjamin has become fully Canaanite (even Sodomite). So, when Israel asks for a king "to judge us like all the nations" (1 Sam. 8:5), we should be horrified with the selection of Saul, a man from the tribe of Benjamin, from the town of Gibeah. If there is ever a king who ironically fulfills the people's request, it is Saul (whose name means "asked for"), a king like the nations' but not a king after God's own heart.

> ## Theological Soundings

GOD-TALK AND THE THIRD COMMANDMENT. The Third Commandment forbids the misuse of God's name: "You shall not take [lift up] the name of the LORD your God in vain, for the LORD will not hold him guiltless who takes his name in vain" (Ex. 20:7). We have come narrowly to think that the breaking of this command occurs mainly in the use of certain modern expletives. But there are much subtler and more dangerous ways to misuse the name and reputation of God. We see such instances here in Judges 18, when a false priest provides a false affirmation in the name of God: "Go in peace. The journey on which you go is *under the eye of the* LORD" (v. 6); or when the scouts return from Laish and state, "for *God* has given it into your hands" (v. 10). Consider how the name of God is used to validate or even spiritualize the unsanctioned and illicit activity of the tribe of Dan. We are in danger of doing the very same thing when we act in ways contrary to the revealed Word of God yet seek to justify it with our God-talk. We may say something like, "I know this must be the *will of God* for my life," even when we are unsure or know it isn't true. We must guard our words and not impugn the character of God with vain God-talk.

THE HORROR OF SIN. The accounts recorded in Judges 17–21 are shocking in content and detail, and these chapters were intended by God to provoke this reaction. We should appreciate that the Bible, particularly the book of Judges, has not been sanitized or cleaned up. Scripture depicts real life, including some of the very worst parts of life in this world. For example, Eglon is slain and lies dead in his own excrement. Abimelech executes 70 of his brothers on a single rock in a single day. Brutal acts such as sodomy, gang rape, and mutilation are not overlooked. Behavior of this type is horrific and abominable in the eyes of God, but he has not shied away from including this content in his Holy Word, so that we might be jolted awake and made to understand the hideous horror of sin. "Wretched man that I am!" the apostle Paul declared as he reflected on his own sinfulness, "Who will deliver me from this body of death? Thanks be to God through Jesus Christ our Lord!" (Rom. 7:24–25).

▶ **Personal Implications**

Take time to reflect on the implications of Judges 17:1–21:25 for your life. How does this passage lead you to praise God, repent of sin, and trust more deeply in his gracious promises? Write down your reflections under the three headings we have considered and on the passage as a whole.

1. Gospel Glimpses

2. Whole-Bible Connections

3. Theological Soundings

4. Judges 17:1–21:25

> ### As You Finish This Unit . . .

Take a few minutes to ask for God's help to grasp the significance of these difficult narratives for the Christian life. Do not despair. In these days there is a King, and he has done all that is right in the Father's eyes. He now lives and reigns forever over a people rescued from the type of horrors narrated in Judges 17–21.

WEEK 12: SUMMARY AND CONCLUSION

We will conclude our study of the book of Judges by summarizing the big picture of God's message through Judges as a whole. Then we will consider several questions in order to reflect on various *Gospel Glimpses*, *Whole-Bible Connections*, and *Theological Soundings* throughout the entire book.

The Big Picture of Judges

The framework in which the judge narratives are placed sets before our eyes the terror of forgetting the God of our salvation and his relentless mercy to bring us back to himself. Over and over again, God's people forget, forsake, and do evil. Remember the repeated description of this period: "In those days there was no king in Israel. Everyone did what was right in his own eyes" (Judg. 17:6; compare 18:1; 19:1; 21:25). But Israel's sin is forever outpaced by God's redeeming grace as he raises up judges to deliver his people from their idolatry and foreign subjugation.

In the book of Judges, we see ourselves in the nation of Israel. We are the ones who have repeatedly done evil in the sight of God as we struggle to remember the covenantal grace of the gospel. The book of Judges also teaches us that since we are sinners, we definitely need a savior like the ones raised up by God in this book. Remember that the book of Hebrews teaches us how to think about these kingdom servants:

> Time would fail me to tell of *Gideon, Barak, Samson, Jephthah,* of David and Samuel and the prophets—who *through faith* conquered kingdoms, enforced justice, obtained promises, stopped the mouths of lions, quenched the power of fire, escaped the edge of the sword, were made strong out of weakness, became mighty in war, put foreign armies to flight. (Heb. 11:32–34)

These temporary saviors forever point beyond themselves to the one true Savior. The judges were "commended though their faith" (Heb. 11:39) and are now part of that "great . . . cloud of witnesses" (Heb. 12:1) who together now call us to fix our eyes on Jesus (Heb. 12:2), the true and better Judge!

▶ Gospel Glimpses

To borrow from the apostle Paul, the book of Judges constitutes the gospel "promised beforehand" (Rom. 1:2). These narratives put on full display the repeated sin of God's people and the relentless mercy of God to save by raising up judges through whom he rescues his people. As Israel's sin increases, so does their oppression. As their oppression increases, so does the cost of the judge to save. By the end of the book we should be asking ourselves, What could God ever do that would stop this cycle of sin and forever deliver his people? The answer is that God appeared himself in the person of Jesus in order to pay the ultimate price and reign forever so that our obedience is secured and our inheritance guaranteed. Because "it is finished" (John 19:30), the gospel is good news.

How has the book of Judges brought new clarity to your understanding of the gospel?

What particular passages or themes in Judges have led you to a fresh understanding and grasp of God's grace to us through Jesus?

Whole-Bible Connections

The book of Judges represents an important link in the history of redemption, which stretches from the first chapters of Genesis to the new creation in Revelation. Judges is anchored to the book of Joshua, as it opens with the account of Joshua's death, which takes us back to Moses, thus grounding the book in the covenant made at Sinai. But the book of Judges also points us forward to the books of Samuel and Kings as we anticipate God's solving the problem of leadership demonstrated in the book of Judges ("there was no king in Israel"). The themes of idolatry, sin, oppression, rescue, and kingship run across the pages of Scripture, connecting each book of the Bible to one another as the inspired Word comes to full expression in the Incarnate Word, Jesus Christ.

How has this study of Judges amplified your understanding of the biblical storyline of redemption?

What themes emphasized in Judges helped you deepen your grasp of the Bible's unity?

What passages or themes expanded your understanding of the redemption Jesus provides, begun at his first coming and to be consummated at his return?

What connections between Judges and the New Testament were new to you?

▶ Theological Soundings

The book of Judges amply contributes to the categories of Christian theology. Numerous doctrines, themes, and ethical standards are developed and reinforced in this oft-neglected book of the Old Testament. We have encountered the corruption of sin and the breaking of covenant, the anger and mercy of God, the hope of a savior, the possibility of a king, the need of repentance, and the joy of obedience. The book of Judges presents to us "theology in action."

Has your theology, or the way in which you think theologically, shifted in minor or major ways during the course of studying Judges? How so?

How has your understanding of the nature and character of God been deepened throughout this study?

What unique contributions does Judges make toward our understanding of who Jesus is and what he accomplished through his life, death, and resurrection?

What specifically does Judges teach us about the human condition and our need of redemption?

Personal Implications

The book of Judges was ultimately written to testify to the person and work of Jesus (John 5:39) in order to produce in us the obedience of faith (Rom. 1:5). Understand, then, that the book of Judges was not written only to change your mind. It was written to change your life. The often shocking nature of the judge narratives were written in this way to arrest your attention and to bring you into the presence of the God of your salvation; to come with unveiled face, to behold the glory of the Lord, and to be "transformed into the same image from one degree of glory to another" (2 Cor. 3:18).

God wrote the book of Judges to transform you. As you reflect on Judges as a whole, what implications do you see for your life?

What implications for life flow from your reflections on the questions already asked in this week's study concerning *Gospel Glimpses, Whole-Bible Connections,* and *Theological Soundings?*

What have you learned in Judges that might lead you to praise God, turn away from sin, and trust more firmly in his promises?

As You Finish Studying Judges . . .

We rejoice with you as you finish studying the book of Judges! May this study become part of your Christian walk of faith, day by day and week by week throughout all your life. Now we would greatly encourage you to study the Word of God on a week-by-week basis. To continue your study of the Bible, we would encourage you to consider other books in the *Knowing the Bible* series and visit www.knowingthebible.org.

Lastly, take a moment to look back through this study. Review the notes that you have written and the things that you have highlighted or underlined. Reflect again on the key themes that the Lord has been teaching you about himself and about his Word. May these things become a treasure for you throughout your life—this we pray in the name of the Father and the Son and the Holy Spirit. Amen.